O Holy Spirit, Enlighten Me

I. M. FREE

ISBN 978-1-956696-25-7 (paperback)
ISBN 978-1-956696-26-4 (hardcover)
ISBN 978-1-956696-27-1 (digital)

Copyright © 2021 by I. M. Free

All rights reserved. No part of this publication may be reproduced, distributed, or transmitted in any form or by any means, including photocopying, recording, or other electronic or mechanical methods without the prior written permission of the publisher. For permission requests, solicit the publisher via the address below.

Rushmore Press LLC
1 800 460 9188
www.rushmorepress.com

Printed in the United States of America

To David Cole

Without David's thoughtful and encouraging words, this book might never have been released in my lifetime. It was one thing to open my soul to friends and acquaintances, but sharing my experiences with the public was not an easy decision for me.

Table of Contents

Keynote.................................... vii
Introduction ix

Chapter 1 1
Chapter 2 6
Chapter 3 16
Chapter 4 27
Chapter 5 36
Chapter 6 45
Chapter 7 52
Chapter 8 59
Chapter 9 64
Chapter 10 71
Chapter 11 79
Chapter 12 86
Chapter 13 94

PART 2

Chapter 14 105
Chapter 15 113
Chapter 16 118

Chapter 17	125
Chapter 18	133
Chapter 19	138
Chapter 20	145
Chapter 21	152
Chapter 22	158
Chapter 23	166
Chapter 24	173
Chapter 25	182
Chapter 26	193
Chapter 27	198
Chapter 28	207
Chapter 29	215
Chapter 30	218
Chapter 31	228
Chapter 32	235
Chapter 33	242

Keynote

I awoke with a message from God. During my sleep, He explained the signs of the cross. Catholics repeat the signs of the cross, "In the name of the Father, the Son, and the Holy Spirit."

God said to me, "What we think (touch the forehead), what we eat (touch the stomach), and what we do (touch one shoulder and then the other), all must be in harmony."

Before we can hear God and truly follow Him and not ourselves, all of these things must be in order.

Introduction

Some people are born knowing there is a God. I was not one of them. As a child, I questioned the stories I had heard. I couldn't accept there was a being with that much control over our lives. The thought of someone taking it upon himself to build an ark and fill it with animals was beyond my imagination. This couldn't be true. How could people believe this?

As a nonbeliever, when I began having visions in my mind that I didn't understand, I began questioning what I was experiencing. I wondered: why was this happening to me? I realized I was experiencing something none of my friends had experienced. In my mind, I began hearing answers to my questions. I began to understand I was not alone. Something was really guiding me and knew what I was going to do before I did it.

When I tried to explain to others what was happening to me, no one could understand. I realized I was different. But I was the only one who knew it was a good kind of different.

I. M. Free

After some time, I would realize I was communicating with God. Since the beginning of time, only a select few have been able to hear God. I found out that I was one of them. I now understood why Noah built an ark. I knew he had been following that silent voice in his head.

I was in my early thirties when I became aware of something guiding me. Once I became aware of that guidance, I couldn't put it out of my life. It became my life.

I have friends who believe they have found God, yet when I say I hear God, they can't comprehend how this is possible. I do hear God. I hear Him when I am truly at peace with myself. He prepares me for the things that are going to most challenge me or change my life.

Sometimes when I awaken, I know something I didn't before I fell asleep. I feel things I wasn't even aware I knew. God has given me the gift of understanding why some things happened in the past or other events are going to occur in the future. This is how God protects me and prepares me for life.

I felt the most traumatic events in my life prior to their happening. I don't always understand the message when I receive it, but I've learned I must be patient. When He is ready, I will understand.

When I found God, one of my first messages was, "Put nothing between you and Me." Why would God instruct me to put nothing between Him and myself? Believing God gave me this message for a reason, I have never followed the Bible, even though I know it is full of good.

In the beginning, there was no Bible. They had nothing to follow except their own instincts. When I look at how our moral values have changed in my lifetime, how can I trust the Bible is truly God's actual Word? God did not write the

O Holy Spirit, Enlighten Me

Bible. Isn't it possible, even then, our moral values changed significantly from the time of Jesus and when the Bible was written?

I've watched persons in my life follow the Bible, trusting it was guiding them in the right direction. I can't do that. It is my belief, all too often, this is Satan's opening, and we will be misguided. Satan is extremely clever. God speaks to me without consulting the Bible. Again His words to me were, "Put nothing between you and me."

Believing the only way to truly follow God is through listening to the guiding voice in my head, it is the only thing I completely trust and believe. Sometimes the message can come from something I see or hear or even the mouth of another. Once the message is delivered, that voice guides me and helps me make the decisions with which I can live. I don't get immediate answers to my questions, but I've learned that I must be patient. In time, I will receive an answer, even though it isn't always the one I wanted to receive. When you receive your answer, it comes with an inner peace, and you then know He has answered you. It has been a long and slow road, but it is so worth the time. My faith has only grown stronger with time.

God has given me the gift of inner peace. As long as I have that, I haven't let the devil tempt or misguide me. If I am not at peace with myself, it can only be that I have let myself become distracted and lost my way. It is then I have to communicate with the voice in my head, and He points out my indiscretion.

God guides me in what I say, do, and eat. I pay the price when I choose not to listen. No one else experiences the consequences. If I should say or do something that is wrong and am aware of my indiscretion and choose not to resolve it, my inner peace is gone. I risk my health. The body functions best when we have inner peace.

It doesn't matter how we find God, only that we do. I believe, if you really want to communicate with God, the first step must be to open your mind. You must put the Bible aside and communicate with God directly. Get in touch with yourself.

Many Christians seem to believe God favors those who follow the Bible and go to church regularly. I do neither. Organized religion turns me off. Each religion believes its beliefs are the right ones. I can't follow someone else's beliefs. I have to be free to follow what my conscience is telling me is right for me.

God is alive and present today, as He was thousands of years ago. And today, as then, most are unable to hear Him. Busy with their everyday lives, they don't listen to the voice in their head, trying to be heard. Concentrating on other things, they have unconsciously closed their minds to God.

Trying to be good Christians, people devote their lives to seeking and praising God. They go to church, pray, and read the Bible. Many are searching outside themselves instead of listening to the silent voice inside their head. Despite their attempts to find God, they never open their mind and let Him in. And because God communicates with us through our mind, until they open their mind, they can't possibly hear Him.

I believe I can hear God because I have an open mind, a clear conscience, and a good heart, not because I am perfect. I know I am not perfect, but I am constantly trying to become a better person. Right or wrong, I try to be as honest as I can be. Tonight, God may tell me I was wrong. Tomorrow, I may see something differently, but today, you will get an honest answer.

When it comes to religion, most do not want to hear anything beyond what they have been taught or believe presently. They won't go beyond their comfort zone or even consider anything that goes against what their present religion represents. That is not having an open mind.

Having observed others for much of my life, it is my belief we are brainwashed from the time we are old enough to learn. We may not want to hear this or see it, but our religious beliefs and discriminations are two areas of major brainwashing.

If we could erase everything we have ever been taught or overheard, what would we really believe? If we had no previous teaching of religion, we would have to listen to our conscience. "Let your conscience be your guide."

The God I hear and follow loves everyone. God understands why we feel and act as we do. Being a truly loving God, He will give us as many lifetimes as we need to work out our misjudgments.

The discrimination against black people is an excellent example of discrimination passed down generation after generation. When does it stop? My God isn't sitting in judgment of someone should he or she choose to love someone of the same sex. Some of the most beautiful, generous, talented persons on this earth are gay. So what! Why does this bother many who believe they are good Christians but sit in judgment of others?

Whether Christian, Jewish, Muslim, Buddhist, and so on, all too often, we are mere extensions of our roots.

I. M. Free

Unfortunately many will never grow beyond what they have been taught or overheard as children. No wonder it takes years and years for change to occur. I find this so sad because it is my belief we are all following the same God.

When a person finds and hears God is entirely between God and that person, no one else can make it happen. God has a plan for each of us. He knows what we are going to do before we do it. He knows exactly how long it is going to take us to find our path.

Chapter 1

The day started as any other day. I was home, cleaning my house and enjoying the freedom of being a homemaker. Suddenly there was a loud explosion, and my house and windows shook. At the same time as the explosion, there was what I describe as a flash in my mind. The flash told me someone was going to be killed in an automobile accident. For some unknown reason, I looked at the clock. It was two forty-two in the afternoon.

When I later asked my neighbors if they had heard the explosion, no one knew what I was talking about. Not one person heard an explosion. No other houses shook. When I explained to friends what had happened, including the vision, several tried to convince me I had imagined the entire thing. But I knew I hadn't imagined it. When it happened, my body felt sad, as though I had lost someone. The entire thing was very real to me and upset me terribly.

About one month later, while a friend was visiting at my house, again there was an explosion. My house shook, and again I had a flash in my mind. Again the flash told me someone was going to be killed in an accident. It was two forty-two in the afternoon.

My friend also heard the explosion and said, "Yes, the house did shake."

It was proof I had not imagined this. Again my body felt sad, as though I had already lost someone.

For months, this was something I would often talk about with friends. It really upset me, and no one could explain why this happened or what it meant. I wanted someone to say, "Yes, something like that happened to me."

But no one had ever experienced anything like what I was talking about. Not one person knew anyone to whom something like this had happened.

Later that same year, I awoke in the morning with the feeling someone close to me had passed away. For days, my body would feel deep sorrow, as though someone had already died and I was in mourning. Then after three or four days, the mood would lift, and I would feel as though I were pregnant.

Again I spoke to anyone who would listen about what was occurring in my body. No one could explain what was happening. I so wanted to find someone who had experienced something similar and could explain what was happening. I knew I wasn't imagining these things. They were very real.

With the new awareness happening in my body, I began to listen to what my body was telling me. I was playing tennis three or four days a week. I had never been conscious about my diet. I was always an active person. I had two kids and helped my husband build three homes. But time was catching up with me. I found I could no longer work nonstop. After tennis, I was totally exhausted, unable to do anything except rest. I used to clean my house in a day. Now I could only work for a very short period of time, and I had to sit down. Since I was unable to bounce back, my doctor scheduled a test for hypoglycemia. It was a five-hour test.

As I sat in the doctor's office, awaiting the results, a lady was playing with a deck of cards. She asked if she could read my fortune with the cards. Never one to believe this sort of thing, I said "Okay."

As she read the cards, I could not believe what I was hearing. She stated, "Someone you know is going to be killed in an automobile accident. She went on, "You are going to lose someone close to you. This is going to upset you very much. The person has dark brown hair." Her words really surprised me. She had just repeated my visions to me. There was no way she could have known about my previous revelations.

Even before my visions, I had feared for my father and his driving. My father was an alcoholic. I had always feared he would kill, either himself or someone else, while driving drunk. Not understanding what God was trying to tell me, I believed the two visions must be one event. But I couldn't be sure. I would ask my conscience over and over again, "What are you trying to tell me?"

Those visions would take over my life. I was constantly trying to figure out what was happening. I couldn't let go of it. I knew I was going to lose someone whom I cared about, and that troubled me greatly.

After much thought and the passage of time, I realized my father no longer had brown hair. His hair was now gray. It was not my father.

While dating my husband, I had joined the Catholic Church. Even though I attended church every week for nearly fifteen years, I never felt a connection to the church. It was something I did to appease my husband. I was not sure I believed in God. In fact, I would have said, "No, I don't believe in God."

Now years later, I knew something was guiding me, something of which I had never been aware. I now know there is a God and He is aware of my deepest fears, one of which is the death of someone close to me. I knew I was being prepared for something that would change my life forever. Wanting to understand what God was trying to divulge to me, it was my belief He was telling me this person's soul was going to be reborn to me, which was why I always felt pregnant after experiencing the death.

I am certain everyone thought I was having a nervous breakdown, but I knew what I was feeling was real. I was certain someone I cared about was going to leave me. I knew because my body had already begun mourning. And because the person was close to me and had dark brown hair, if it weren't my father, I began to believe it was my tennis buddy. I was probably with her four days a week, playing tennis.

My friend was a happy person. She made me laugh like no one I had ever known. She was a very good person. Both of us were very competitive when it came to tennis. I had some of the best times of my life with her. Although she was more than ten years younger than I was, we seemed to have a lot in common. Both of us loved our tennis. It would have upset me terribly to lose her.

Before I became hypoglycemic, I had never paid attention to my body. Fortunately, even though I had terrible eating habits, I had always been healthy. For years, I had lived on junk food and pop. Now since I had depleted my body of

O Holy Spirit, Enlighten Me

many necessary nutrients, my body broke down. I now had to listen to my body.

As I learned to listen to my conscience, I was guided to reading materials that would help me understand my body and what I was lacking. My eating habits changed dramatically. I avoided sugar as much as possible. I had always eaten too much sugar. It seemed, the less sugar I ate, the more relaxed my body became. And the more relaxed I became, the more psychic I became. Months later, I unexpectedly became pregnant, and my visions would again dominate my thoughts.

Believing the person I was going to lose would be reborn to me, I was certain I would lose my friend before the baby was born. I know it sounds crazy, even to me. But that was what was on my mind. As I went into labor months later, I was especially stressed.

Whatever God was trying to tell me, it wasn't that I was going to lose my friend. I gave birth, and thank God, my friend was still here. I was driving myself crazy trying to figure out what my visions were all about. I was certain there was a reason I had gone through this. For the life of me, I just couldn't figure it out.

Chapter 2

It has been more than forty years since I experienced my visions. God has since explained each, and having experienced them so long beforehand made it so much easier to accept when they actually happened. For me, the visions were the beginning of my life. I assume this is what they mean when they talk about someone being reborn. It took God shaking my house and planting a vision in my mind before I opened my mind and was able to see the light.

One doesn't become a good person just because he or she has found God. It takes many years of conscience examination of previous bad decisions. Eventually you decide you can do better, and you gradually change the person inside of you. At least that is the way it was for me.

When I look back over my life, certain moments will always remain in my mind. I have to go back to the beginning to really appreciate how far I have come in this lifetime. Recalling my childhood, before elementary school, was a

O Holy Spirit, Enlighten Me

happy time. We lived in a very small, isolated neighborhood of about six homes. Except for one family, we were all related.

My grandfather's farm was the first home, and the family built additional homes around the farm. Some were from my mother's side of the family; others were from my father's side of the family. I would spend my childhood playing with my cousins and the three unrelated neighbor boys. Those were the good old days, spent playing games outside in the fresh air or building huts in the straw or hay in my grandfather's barn. Life was good.

Feeling secure in our small neighborhood, when I began my first year of school, I didn't want to leave home. Because I can remember things that happened in the first grade, I am aware of how even the smallest event can remain with us forever. For me, one of those events would probably be meaningless to most but is probably the most special moment I can remember between my older sister and myself.

My first grade teacher had a rule, "Drink your milk or no recess." Having swallowed sour white milk too often at home, I could drink chocolate milk, but not white. Sometimes I had no choice but to take the white milk. For me, this meant no recess.

Knowing my predicament, my older sister Pat would stop by my classroom on her way to recess and drink my milk so I might go outside with the other kids. Sadly, because my sister and I would grow up constantly bickering with one another, this is one of the most loving memories I have of her. This would be before both of us decided we didn't like one another. As we grew older, we would never become close.

Today when I think of Pat, I wonder where she was while the rest of us were outside playing. She was never with us. I have no idea where she was. Now, many years later, I wonder what she was doing.

In the second grade, my closest friend was moving away at the end of the school year. I was devastated. Much more aware of the direct connection between my emotions and my health, I truly believe this was a contributing factor in my becoming ill with scarlet fever.

My next memorable event would be in the fifth grade. I had been held over for a music lesson in another part of the school and was late getting back to class. Obviously the teacher believed I was late because I chose to be late, and having already given the class the instructions for the test, she was not about to repeat anything. Because I underlined the answers instead of circling them, I flunked the exam.

Always a good student, as a fifth grader, I found the entire situation very upsetting. I had done nothing wrong, but the teacher obviously did not believe me and was not about to change my grade. The lessons I learned from this teacher were not positive. I learned at a very young age that sometimes you just can't win. To this day, I know there are some who just shouldn't be teaching. Even as small children, we begin to make observations about life and to shape the person we are to become.

When I entered junior high school, my life would begin to change. My personality began to transform. I would lose touch with most of the girls with whom I had been friends all through elementary school. I instead chose a select few, who have remained in my circle to this day. If I had it to do over again, I would not have ignored the many friends I had before becoming part of a clique.

O Holy Spirit, Enlighten Me

The good, happy days would become a memory. My grades would begin to dip somewhat. It became harder to concentrate on schoolwork. School was no longer my priority. My home life would dominate my thoughts.

Life at home would never again be as I'd once remembered it. If there had been problems previously, I hadn't noticed. But now things were so out of control that I couldn't ignore it. These days, it seemed my father was always in a bad mood. He was seldom home for dinner, and when he was, it was unpleasant. Tension filled every day at our house.

Dad had quit his regular job and was now a self-employed plumber. This left him to do what he wanted when he wanted. And what he wanted to do most these days was drink. Between his drinking and his hobby, which was boating, it seemed there was never enough money to make ends meet at our house. As a result, my mother worked most of the time. She made sure the utility bills got paid. Seldom was any money left for unnecessary things.

Dad usually did not come home until after the local tavern closed. When he came through the door, it was routine for my parents to have yet another fight over his drinking and money. At least four nights a week, this would be our life.

It would be two in the morning, and the screaming would go on and on. My sisters and I were upstairs and could hear everything. I couldn't imagine what it was like for my brother, Bud. He was in the room downstairs, next to Mom and Dad. My brother is four years younger than I am, and I was having a hard time dealing with our environment. What was this doing to him?

After only a short night's sleep, my mother would get up and go to work. My sisters, brother, and I would get up and go to school. My father would be sound asleep. He would wake when he felt like it. Tonight or the next, we would do it all over again.

With our sleep interrupted more often than not, it was taking a toll on all of us. Only someone who has grown up in an alcoholic household can truly understand. Until you have lived with this day after day, month after month, and year after year, you do not know what it does to you. It leaves scars that, for some, will never be healed. To this day, I will not drink, and I am very uncomfortable around someone when I know he or she is under the influence of alcohol.

About the only time there was money for extras at our house was when my grandfather would give my mother some. This would happen on several occasions, and he would give Mom a substantial amount. This was when we would get a new car or replace the worn-out furniture.

As very young children, we never took a family vacation. Mom and Dad would occasionally get away for a few days alone, but Dad never wanted to take his kids along. He preferred to leave us home or with one of their friends.

As we got older, because the most important thing in my father's life was his boat, we would go boating as often as he could get away. For me, the rides to and from the lake were always stressful. My eyes were always glued to the road in front of us. My father thought he had to pass everyone on the road. He had no patience. With four kids in the car and pulling a boat, he had to be the lead vehicle. He couldn't follow anyone.

As we got older, instead of the local lakes, we would often go to Lake Erie. I never thought of our trips to Lake Erie as a vacation. Pitching a tent, sleeping on the ground, cooking on a camp stove, and showering in a public shower were not my idea of a vacation. This was dirty and more work than staying home.

Although my dad had a boat for most of my childhood, I was never once given the opportunity to try skiing behind that boat. As a family, we seldom went for a boat ride. Dad didn't think about his kids. It was all about him. He needed to get away and relax. We would be left to swim at the state park.

Although we had gone to the lake for the weekend, next week Mom and Dad would fight because there wasn't any money to pay for the groceries, the utilities, or his plumbing supply bills.

As I entered junior high, for a few short years, my father surprisingly abandoned his trips to the lake and his boating. He had decided to build a custard stand across the street from the local beach. During the spring and summer hours, my mother would work daily from eleven in the morning until close. My sister and I would rotate. We either worked from ten or eleven till five in the afternoon or five in the afternoon till close. During the summer vacation, we worked seven days a week. While we worked, my father would be across the street, at the local tavern. He was seldom involved with the custard stand. For the summer's work, I received two bathing suits and a pass to the beach. We didn't receive an allowance or a wage.

I enjoyed my time at the beach. That was where my friends were, and I wanted to be with them. When not doing the laundry, cleaning the house, or working at the custard stand, I would be at the beach. In my spare time, I babysat for spending money.

I. M. Free

By the time I began my freshman year in high school, I could no longer hide my dislike for my father. It was written all over my face every time I looked at him. I had zero respect for him. He would so often stumble into the house, unable to walk straight or talk without garbling his words. He would find something he wasn't happy about in the house and start an argument with my mother, my brother, or myself. He left my sisters alone. They were smart enough to keep their mouths shut. My mother, brother, and I couldn't. We'd give him the argument he wanted. I was often getting slapped because of a look on my face. I couldn't help it. My feelings and disrespect were written there for him to see, as clear as day.

I hated the way he treated my mother. He called her names I felt she didn't deserve. How could she crawl into bed with him night after night? Why did she let him degrade her in front of others by putting his hands in her clothes or in places that belonged in the bedroom between only the two of them? Why did my mother stay?

I was disgusted as I watched my father answer the phone in the dining room, stark naked. We girls were in high school. What was wrong with this man? I would never understand why he was so nasty to all of us. God, I hated him.

I believe we were in the second year of running the custard stand when we were having a particularly hot spell. For days, the temperature was in the nineties. I asked my sister if she would take my swimsuit to the custard stand with her so I wouldn't have to carry it when I walked to work. The custard stand was about one mile from our house. It wasn't a big deal. She could leave it in the car.

My father overheard me ask her to take the swimsuit. He started yelling at me, "The custard stand is not a beach

O Holy Spirit, Enlighten Me

house. You can carry the damn thing down when you come down."

What was the big deal? Again, I couldn't believe my ears. He was screaming over my bathing suit being at the custard stand. That was just how crazy our life had become.

Feeling totally disgusted with my father, I headed for the basement. It was my turn to do the laundry. As I went down the stairs, I ever so softly mumbled one word, "queer." Unknown to me, my father had moved to the top of the stairs and overheard me.

He flew down those stairs and began beating me in a way he had never hit me before. He was like a crazy man. He had his arm around my body until my mouth was at his back. He was really hurting me, and I had to defend myself as best as I could. Unable to do anything else, I bit him in his back as hard as I could.

For the first and only time in her life, my mother got between my father and me. I am certain she was afraid for me, or she would not have gotten involved. When I said "queer," I meant it as odd or stupid. I certainly wasn't calling my father a queer.

When my father died many years later, he still had my teeth prints in his back. I would never feel guilty for biting him. I felt I hadn't done anything to deserve the beating I got that day. The whole thing was crazy.

When the custard stand was closed for the season, we were back to our usual routine. Mom was working another job, we were in school, and Dad was drinking.

One of my classmates asked me out. I was dressed and waiting for him to pick me up. When my father came home, we got into our usual argument over nothing. He screamed at me, "You are not going anywhere. Get to your room."

I stated, "I am going out. I need to call my date and tell him I can't go."

Dad wouldn't hear of it. "Get to your room!" Being his usual unreasonable self, as the only phone was in the dining room downstairs, I was unable to call my date.

I went to my room as ordered. I couldn't let my date come to the house to pick me up. Who knew what sort of scene Dad would create? I had to call my date. Not knowing what else to do, I climbed out my bedroom window and down the television antenna tower. I went to my aunt's house to make the phone call. By the time I returned, Dad had passed out and never knew I left the house. Although Dad would often show an affectionate side to the children of friends, we never saw that side of him. So often I feared my mother, brother, or I could have killed him. He pushed us that far.

I was so tired of our home life. It had been going on for years. I couldn't foresee it ever changing. I began to ask myself, "What is life all about?" I could see no purpose. I couldn't remember when I last felt happy. It had been years of fighting, fighting, and more fighting. There was no place to go to escape.

Feeling I couldn't cope with any more screaming, fighting, and anger and was unable to see anything beyond our miserable life, I decided I just didn't want to be here anymore. All of this was because of my father's need to drink. I felt certain life was never going to change.

Alone in my room, I took a razor and scratched my wrist. I was sitting and looking at the scratch, preparing to do it again, except harder. Suddenly an unexplained peace took over my body.

A voice in my head said, "Don't do it. One day you will have children and a home."

It was so strange. I had never experienced anything like this before. It made me stop and think. I put the razor down and never contemplated anything like that again. I never forgot what happened; nor did I in any way connect what had just happened to God. After all, I didn't believe in Him.

Chapter 3

As I entered my senior year of high school, my relationship with my father hadn't changed one bit. Although I didn't lie, skip school, steal, smoke cigarettes, do drugs, drink, or have premarital sex, I was always in trouble. My sin was that I hated my father and I wasn't capable of hiding it from him. I had finally reached the point where I just wouldn't make eye contact with my father. In fact, I tried to stay out of his space altogether.

It bothered me that I hated him. I worried he would die and I'd have to live with the fact I hated him so much. I would never be able to make things right between us. Our relationship wasn't the way I wanted it, but I just couldn't help how I felt. But my fear didn't change my feelings. They were that deep. How could I pretend I loved and respected someone whom I so much despised?

I had watched my father mistreat my mother for years. I would never understand why she stayed, except she couldn't afford to leave him. And I was certain she would not have left her children with him. Did she really love him? How could she?

Halfway through my senior year, my next-door neighbor told me her nephew had seen my senior picture. He wanted her to arrange a date. Although I had never met her nephew, I remembered watching him play basketball when I was a freshman. A senior at the time, he was on the varsity basketball team. I knew he was also very good at football. I remembered watching him and only him as he played basketball and thinking how cute I thought he was. I was really flattered he would be interested in taking me out.

When I met Dick, he was recuperating from a work-related injury. He had serious surgery on his knee, and while so many guys his age were being drafted into the service, this would keep him from entering the service.

Once Dick and I began dating, I never went out with anyone else. I was still interested in a couple of other guys, but when told we were through if I dated anyone else, I didn't test him. Years later, as I looked back over my life, I would believe this was a mistake on my part. He now knew he could control me somewhat.

We had been dating for some time. We were watching television one evening when my father came home. Dad, as usual, had been drinking and was stumbling and slurring his words. Suddenly I was being sent to my room. This time I didn't even remember what upset him. Whatever it was, I didn't feel I had done anything that deserved being sent to my room. I was eighteen years old and would be graduating soon.

I couldn't believe my father acted like he did, and I was even more surprised when Dick said nothing. He just got up and left for home. I was as disappointed in Dick as I was angry at my father. At the time, I told myself that Dick didn't come to my defense because he didn't want to create a scene with my father. I failed to see to whom I was making a lifelong commitment.

Not long after I graduated from high school, while I was relaxing at home, the phone rang. Mom and Dad were, as they often were, at Lake Erie. It was my younger sister Carol. She had gone away with her boyfriend, who had just graduated with me.

She proudly announced, "Chuck and I just got married."

My response was, "You idiot! What did you do that for?"

Although I was certain Carol loved Chuck, I was also certain Carol had found an out, and Chuck was it. Living at our house was not fun. She had done something I would never have dreamed of going through with. Carol hadn't yet finished high school. But to her credit, even though she was married, she would finish school. The marriage, however, did not last. Many years later, I would discover Carol was as addicted to alcohol as our father was. It is something with which she would struggle her entire life.

About this time, my father's sister revealed to us that we had a sister. Unknown to us, our father had a wife before our mother. He had abandoned that family and come to Ohio, where he would eventually meet and marry my mother.

It seems a girl convinced my grandparents she was pregnant with my father's baby. Doing the proper thing, my grandparents made my father marry the girl, only to find she wasn't pregnant at the time. But she did become pregnant soon after the marriage. Although that doesn't excuse my father for his bad choices, I was beginning to understand why my father was so troubled. He definitely had to feel he had been wronged.

My father had come to Ohio and worked on my grandfather's farm, which was how he met my mother. My father married my mother when she became pregnant. Was this why he called my mother some of the names he did? Did he feel he had been trapped again? Did he not want to have children? Was this why he seemed angry all the time? Understanding life had not been good to him, I am far from forgiving him, but I am trying. After all, he had done it all to himself.

Most of what I learned about my parents would come from my aunt. My parents didn't talk about their lives. I knew very little about their lives before they became parents. Although they didn't talk about their past, neither did they voice their complaints about one another to us. Of course, they didn't really have to. We were witness to much of their discord. But to their credit, even though they fought constantly, neither would verbalize any complaints about their health or their lives. The fights were most always about my father's drinking and money.

After I graduated from high school, I took a job as a secretary at a small company downtown. I would eventually lose touch with my high school friends, and my world now revolved around the girls with whom I worked and my future husband. By this time, Dick and I had decided we would get married one day.

Wanting to get off to a good start, we saved everything we could. We would pay for most of our wedding ourselves. Dick came from a large family, which included three sisters and three brothers. His mother was a widow. Neither his mother nor my parents had the money for multiple weddings.

Three weeks before our wedding, Dick and I went to a Christmas dance. After a pleasant evening, where Dick obviously had too much to drink, we walked to our car. While waiting for the rest of our group to reach their cars, Dick passed out behind the wheel. Thank goodness we hadn't left the parking lot. One of the other guys moved Dick out of the driver's seat, and I drove to his house.

The next day, totally upset with the previous evening, I told him, "If you are going to drink, don't marry me." I never meant anything more in my life. There was no way on this earth I was going to follow in my mother's footsteps and be married to an alcoholic.

After that, for the most part, Dick would seldom drink more than he could hold. Everyone will slip occasionally. While I kept him from drinking too much, he kept me from beginning to smoke. Although he smoked, he absolutely hated to see a woman with a cigarette in her mouth. This kept me from picking up the habit.

A couple weeks later, on a terrible snowy day in January, we were married. Being two naïve young people, totally oblivious to the weather reports, the next morning we left for Washington, DC, a terrible choice for January. While on the way, our car heater would quit working. It was freezing and snowing.

Upon reaching our destination, we inquired about having our heater repaired. We found we couldn't afford to have the heater checked, let alone repaired.

After a couple days of freezing temperatures, we left Washington, DC, and headed to my grandparents' home in

Pennsylvania. Once there, they directed us to a garage, where we could afford to have our heater repaired.

The funniest event on my honeymoon occurred at my grandparents' home. We were spending the night there. Exhausted from our day's travel, Dick and I had gone upstairs to bed before my grandparents. Unable to get to sleep, we decided we were used to sleeping on the opposite side of the bed.

As we were in the process of crawling over one another to change sides of the bed, my grandparents came up the stairs. This wasn't a box spring type bed. It was the old actual spring-style bed. I don't think I ever heard a bed squeak as loud as the bed we were in that night. To this day, this makes me laugh because I know what my grandmother thought was going on. I never did tell my grandmother what we were actually doing.

After our honeymoon, I returned to work. A few weeks later, I began feeling nauseous. My working career would be short-lived. Since I was newly married, having children hadn't even entered my mind. Before I had time to think about whether I wanted to be a mother, I would become one. Our first girl was born at the end of October.

When my first baby girl was born, I thought she was the cutest baby I'd ever seen. She was adorable. But as I would jokingly say for years and years afterward, she came out of the womb with a mind of her own. If I said "don't do it," it was as though that was all she could think of doing. She would prove to be a challenge for me until she married and left my care.

When we had her baptized, the monsignor didn't like the way I spelled my daughter's name. We had named her Kristina Lynn. He informed me that was not a Christian spelling. I made no attempt to change the spelling of my daughter's name. I had only been a Catholic for a very short time. Since I had not grown up in the Catholic faith, his words irritated me.

After becoming pregnant so easily and quickly, I would ask myself, "Why am I a Catholic?" I believe in birth control. This, along with listening to the monsignor speak about money every Sunday, I was beginning to believe I was in the wrong church. Besides, I was not really sure I believed in God.

Our daughter was barely walking when we decided to build. We bought a lot from Dick's uncle, and with the help of many good friends, we built our first home. No longer doing office work, I thoroughly enjoyed building our home. I would run for supplies, clean up after the workers, assist with the electrical work, pound nails when necessary, and do all the painting, inside and out. It was much more fun than office work. And this felt like the right thing to do. I loved being free to work on my own schedule. Because I didn't have anyone to look after our daughter as I worked on our house, she would be with me all the time.

Two and a half years after the first baby, we had our second daughter. When my first was born, I knew nothing about being a mother. I knew I had made mistakes in raising my first and welcomed the challenge of doing better the second time. And our second child was an angel. She was perfect. She was always pleasant and happy, and unlike her older sister, she never cried. She was a shy little girl, but so precious. We named her Tina Marie. I loved being a mother and had no desire to ever return to the work world. Raising children is work, but I enjoyed the challenge. I felt I was born to be a mother.

The new baby was only a few weeks old when Kris said something to me one day as I was washing dishes in the kitchen. As I turned to look at her, I couldn't believe my eyes. What was she doing? She was not yet three years old, and she was carrying her baby sister. Shocked and not believing she had done this, I didn't say a word. I didn't want to scare Kris. As quickly as I could, I dashed toward her to retrieve the baby.

This would only be the beginning. Kris would require my constant attention most of her childhood. It was not until she was no longer living with us that I could look back at the many memorable moments Kris gave me and appreciate her unique personality. She was an experience I couldn't have survived more than once.

Although my sisters and I have moved out of our family residence, my mother and brother were still home with my father. Things had not improved. In fact, since I had left, my father had been in a couple of bar brawls. Each time he received a black eye, which swelled tremendously. At this time my father would go to the local fishery, purchase a leech, and place it on his face to suck out the excess blood and reduce the swelling. I couldn't look at him when he did this without quivering.

I worried constantly about my mother and her safety. The years of stress were now written all over her face. She was very thin and ill much of the time, but she continued to work. A few times, needing a place to get away, Mom had come and stayed with us for a day or two. Then she would return home. I so wished she would have left my father permanently. Their relationship was so unhealthy. She deserved so much better.

When my mother stayed at my house, I worried my father would come over looking for her. When he was drinking and angry, I was afraid of him. I never knew what he was capable of doing.

When I tried to talk with my husband about my parents, Dick informed me, "I don't want to hear anything about your parents' problems."

His attitude surprised and disappointed me. I would again think about how he had acted years earlier when my father sent me to my room and he had left abruptly. I was beginning to wonder if I had married the wrong person. I believed two married people should know what the other is thinking and feeling. He was supposed to be my best friend, and I couldn't talk to him. This side of him would never change. I realized he really didn't know or care what I was feeling. And for me, this would forever be a wedge between us.

Although Mom and Dad still fought constantly all week, they would also continue to go to Lake Erie as often as they could. By this time, they had graduated from putting up tents to leasing a cabin, and eventually my father had purchased a lot about a quarter mile from the lake and proceeded to build a rather nice cabin, mostly from secondhand materials brought from home. I would never understand how Mom and Dad could fight so much during the week and go to the lake for the weekend, acting like everything was normal. To me, it just never made any sense.

Never one to sit still, while Dick worked all day, I watched our children, mowed the lawn, kept our vehicles clean and polished, and did most of the work the husbands usually do around the house. I didn't mind. I loved doing the work. And this would leave his evenings free to help other friends with their homes, which he often did. I was okay with this, as our friends had helped us.

And because he was gone much of the time, as much as I loved being a mother, there was never a day the girls weren't

O Holy Spirit, Enlighten Me

my responsibility. My husband was a hunter. Every hunting season, he had only one thing on his mind, to head out as often as he could. I looked at this as his vacation. I, on the other hand, would never get a day away from the kids. Dick would never understand that I could also use a break. Because I didn't have a job outside the home, he believed I never did anything. He said every day of my life was a vacation. He didn't believe in taking a vacation. Things hadn't changed since my childhood.

My vacations would still be the weekend. Dick and I would occasionally go to the cabin and visit my parents. If we went to the lake to visit, something always needed to be done around my parents' second home. We would spend our weekend helping them catch up. Again, just as when I was a child, we wouldn't be on the lake.

After seven years in our first home, I became restless to move again. When I suggested building once more, the thought would upset Dick. Any kind of change would always upset Dick. He didn't ever want anything to change. But with a little persistence and after pointing out the financial benefit, we would build our second home. To me, it was fun building because we were doing it together.

We had nearly finished the second house and moved in. We still had things to complete, but at least the house was livable. Dick was working outside, using a pick to dig a drainage line for the downspouts.

The girls were outside with him. He specifically told them, "Don't walk behind me." The words were no more out of his mouth, and Kris, now about eight years old, being her usual self, did not listen.

I. M. Free

Just as he swung the pick, she walked behind him. Unable to stop his swing, he hit her on the top of the head with the tip of the pick. Her head was cut and bleeding, but fortunately, it wasn't a deep cut Knowing she needed to be checked, Dick would be too shook up to accompany us to the hospital. He sent us alone. So Kris and I would drive to the hospital. Upon arriving at the hospital, I would receive the third degree from the hospital staff.

I explained, "My husband hit her in the top of her head with a pick." To make matters worse, this was not Kris's first visit to the hospital.

When Kris was about four, the neighbor was upset with me because I couldn't keep my daughter at home. I had spanked her and told her to stay on the back patio. Never one to like being disciplined, Kris held her breath until she passed out. This time, she went into convulsions.

Not knowing what else to do, I picked her up and ran to the very same neighbor. We worked to get her to come to, after which I took her to the hospital. Kris would be hospitalized for a couple days while they ran tests on her.

When Dick and I visited, she had been put into a crib with a net on top. She wouldn't stay in her crib, so they had attached the net. She didn't heed to the nurses any better than she listened to me. As we walked into her hospital room, she had her hands on the crib bars and was pounding her head on the bars as hard as she could. As a result of that trip, she would be diagnosed as epileptic and would be on medication for a few years.

Now years later, here I was, bringing her back to the hospital with a bleeding head.

Chapter 4

My mother and father decided it was time to let go of our childhood home, as it was more space than they needed. While preparing to sell, my father was working on the lawn and burning weeds and leaves. A lot of smoke was coming from the fire, and the smoke would cover me. Unknown to me, poison ivy was in the fire.

A day after, I knew I was getting poison ivy. Even though no one could see it, I could feel it under my skin. I am very allergic to poison ivy. I have gotten poison ivy in the middle of winter after handling a calamine lotion bottle. So I made an appointment to see the doctor. I wanted him to give me a shot to counteract the poison ivy I knew I was going to get.

At his office, the doctor shared with me it was his first week practicing. The doctor looked at my clear arms, legs, and face and told me, "Go home, take a shower, and don't worry about it." He wouldn't give me a shot. I knew he thought I was crazy. Feeling disappointed, I went home.

Two days later, my hands were swelled up until I couldn't grip a comb to comb my hair. My eyes were tiny slits. I threw a wig on my head and again headed to the doctor. Unable to grip the steering wheel, I had to drive my car with the palms of my hands. Poison ivy now covered me everywhere, except under my panties and bra. Oozing and very swollen, I truly looked like something out of a horror movie.

As I arrived at the doctor's office, they didn't want me to sit in the waiting room. Someone escorted me immediately to the doctor's exam room. This time I would see the senior physician. After he looked at me, he called in the previous doctor to see me. As he entered the room, his eyebrows went up, and his jaw dropped. The look on his face is something I will never forget. My body was swelled so tight that it was hard for me to move. My skin was oozing. If the remedies the doctor gave me didn't work, he said I would have to be hospitalized.

At home, my mother would take the girls, and I would spend a few days in bed, wrapped in white strips of a bed sheet. With arms and legs unable to bend, I looked like a mummy. Since I had previously believed that doctors were always right, this would be my first wake-up moment, and I would realize they do make errors.

After years of feeling I did nothing but work, I found something I enjoyed more than anything I had ever done in my life. I began to play tennis. I never enjoyed anything as much as I enjoyed playing tennis. For me, it opened a whole new world.

Tennis was just beginning to become popular; thus at first there weren't a lot of places to play. At home in the basement, I would spend my time bouncing the ball off

O Holy Spirit, Enlighten Me

the wall, trying to speed up my reaction time. During the winter months, my friend and I would sweep the snow off the outdoor tennis court at a local apartment complex. We would use colored balls so we could find the balls in the snow. I was really hooked.

She and I would eventually sign up for lessons. There, I would meet someone who would become part of my life for many years. There was just something about the instructor's voice. I don't ever remember meeting someone and having the feeling I knew this person before. She had come from another state, so there was no way I had ever run into her before.

My tennis instructor also taught gymnastics, and Kris would become interested. As much as I loved tennis, Kris would love gymnastics. Because the gymnastics classes and indoor tennis courts were in the same facility, it worked out perfectly for us to both to enjoy our newfound hobbies. Tina would try gymnastics, but it wasn't her thing. An especially shy girl, she preferred to stay home. She wasn't outgoing like her older sister.

The cost of gymnastics and tennis would be a problem for my husband. Although I felt we could afford it, Dick didn't believe in spending money you didn't have to spend. He was still in the mode we were in when we were saving to get married. I guess he expected me to save every penny I could for the rest of my life. He would spend much of his time irritated with me because of money, and this part of him would never change.

We just didn't think alike. For example, once I reached my goal, I could loosen the strings and enjoy life. Dick would never share this feeling. Because he was extremely poor as a child, I can understand where he is coming from, but that was then, and this is now.

We had been in our second home only a few short years when I once again got the urge to move one last time. The developer of our allotment had opened a new street. There was a lot on top of a hill that I just loved.

Once again, I started begging my husband to build one more home. With this move, we would have our home paid off. We were young and healthy. Why not? It took a lot more begging than the first time, but I couldn't let go of the urge to build one last time. I felt this was something we really should do. This time, instead of doing most of the work ourselves, we could afford to subcontract more of the work. It would still be work, but not quite as much as the two previous homes had been. Dick reluctantly caved, and even though he didn't want to do it, we would build that third home.

Things didn't go as smoothly this time. There was a building boom at the time, and getting supplies was sometimes impossible. We couldn't get rock lathe to plaster. Then they were plastering the new house, and we still didn't have all the windows. We couldn't get plywood for the subfloor. It was one thing after another. Still I was not sorry we made the move. I knew I was where I wanted to be.

It was hard on Dick, but it was a good move for us. We had a much better lot and house. I have never been sorry we made that last move. I felt like I was home, and I would never suggest building again.

We had been living in our third home for a couple years when I first experienced the visions of which I previously spoke. Dick didn't listen to my rambling about my visions. I'm not sure he ever heard what I was saying. He worked and

O Holy Spirit, Enlighten Me

brought home the money. I paid the bills, cooked the meals, and cared for the kids. He didn't share his feelings and didn't ask about mine. We were like two strangers living together. At the same time, my daughter was still in gymnastics and doing very well. And I was still playing tennis. Both of these things also continued to anger my husband.

At this time, God came into my life. When I look back over my years on this planet, I can understand why He came into my life when He did. Things were going to change dramatically, and I was going to need Him. Once I found God, I began to look at everything in life in a different way. I would realize I had spent most of my life concentrating on myself and what I could do, mostly for myself. I realized there were things about myself I didn't like. I knew I could do better.

No longer thinking only of myself and wanting to do the right thing, I would begin my day asking God what I should do that day. Then I would do whatever it was I felt I was supposed to do. Years later, this would enable me to look back at the past without any regrets. I knew I was following God and this would keep me from ever having any regrets.

With the strain in our marriage, my husband and I were intimate only one time in a year when I became pregnant. It certainly wasn't something I had planned. I was as surprised as anyone. And when I told Dick we were having another baby, he was furious. Our daughters were twelve and nearly fifteen. He didn't want to start over. Once Dick found out we were having another child, the only time he spoke to me during my pregnancy was in the presence of others. It was cold war.

Because of my previous visions, I felt this baby was part of God's plan for us. And I am certain it was, except it would be many years before I would fully understand. Living with the stress brought on by my visions and the lack of communication with my husband, by the time the baby was born, I was ready to divorce my husband and told him so.

Knowing I was not too happy with my marriage, a friend had asked me, "Why do you stay married?"

Because I was asking God every day what I should do, I would realize divorce was not part of God's plan for me. That was not what I was being told to do. With the birth of our third daughter, the stress I felt because of the fear of losing my friend disappeared. I didn't know what God was telling me, but I had to let it go.

Confronted with the realization I'd just about had it with him, Dick would change somewhat. He named the new baby and took an interest in her that he had never shown his first two daughters. For the first time, he became involved and more of a father.

We named our new daughter, Melanie Ann. She was probably the only reason our marriage didn't fall apart. Her sisters, father, and I all adored her. When it came to being good, she even surpassed her sister Tina.

With the help of two sisters, she advanced quickly, and she was walking by nine months. Being a mother for the third time is much easier when you have two teenagers to help with the baby. Her sisters enjoyed her, and I don't think they minded helping.

Unable to forget how their father treated me during the pregnancy, I couldn't let go of my disgust with him. This would prove to be another wedge I wasn't sure I would ever get past. We didn't verbally argue, but a definite distance was between us. It had been years, and he was still pouting about making the third move. Feeling we had done the right thing, I was content in my new environment. I knew I wasn't going to want to move again.

While I was dealing with my small problems, both of my sisters were dealing with their own issues. Carol, who was now living out West, would get breast cancer and have a breast removed. Soon after, she would meet someone new, fall in love, and marry for a second time. My older sister Pat was now married with two small children. Pat would be diagnosed with a cancerous brain tumor. At least it was operable. Pat would have her head shaved and endure brain surgery.

The first time I saw my sister after her surgery, she was in the intensive care unit. Not comfortable with the hospital setting, as I walked into the room, I had never before seen anyone hooked to so many tubes and machines. Her condition shocked me. I felt terrible for her. She looked so weak and fragile.

As I walked across the room to visit, I began to faint. As a paramedic, my brother-in-law was familiar with stressful situations. He obviously recognized the look on my face. I will never know how he crossed that room so quickly and caught me before I hit the floor. Although I felt great sorrow for my sister, I really didn't know what to say, except I was sorry she had to endure this.

Years earlier, shortly after her marriage, Pat had lost her firstborn. She was in the final week of her pregnancy when the baby's umbilical cord wrapped around her neck, and the baby was strangled in the womb. It seemed life was always harder for my older sister.

Melanie was a little over one year old when Kris, Melanie, and I were headed to the store one evening. As I walked to the garage, Dick was outside, talking with his cousin Larry and Larry's next-door neighbor. They had stopped by to visit.

I knew Larry before I met Dick. He too was a cousin to my old next-door neighbors. Years earlier, I had a crush on Larry. I don't think I was ever around Larry when he didn't have a smile on his face. He always seemed to enjoy life. He was a happy, fun-loving guy.

After speaking with them for a few moments, we left and headed to the store. As we were returning home a short time later, we would be the last car to come down the street before the police closed the road. There had been an accident. They weren't letting any more vehicles through. We had no choice but to pull off the road and wait.

As we waited, a paramedic walked past our car. He stated a motorbike had hit a pothole. The bike upset, and the rider's head had hit the bumper of the oncoming car. His brains were all over the road. For some unknown reason, I had a sick feeling that the accident involved Larry.

After I got home, I called another of Dick's cousins and told her there was an accident. I wasn't sure, but I had a feeling it was Larry. I hadn't thought about my vision for quite some time. Could this be what God had warned me about?

I told her, "I think this is the accident I felt a few years earlier when I had my first vision."

I would soon find out it was Larry. Days after his death, my mind would once again begin to wonder, "What exactly was God trying to tell me? Why can't I let go of the other vision?" I now felt certain they must be two separate events.

Sometime after Larry's death, I remembered my own mother had told me that Larry's mother kept going over to the house of her sister, my old next-door neighbor, crying.

She believed Larry was going to be killed on his motorcycle. I hadn't thought about this for years. We don't remember these things because you don't believe they will happen at the time you hear them. It is something I probably would never have recalled, except it did happen. Larry's mother had been right.

Larry's mother would be the only person I ever knew who perhaps could have given me some sort of answer to my visions. Although I knew her, I didn't feel I knew her well enough to approach her about such a sensitive subject.

After she passed, I would forever regret I didn't ask her how she knew.

Chapter 5

One afternoon, Dick, Melanie, and I were sitting on our front porch. Melanie was about two and a half years old. The neighbor kids were playing on our front lawn. We were watching them as they played games and were having a good time.

Distracted, we were unaware Melanie had wandered next door to our neighbors. She couldn't have been gone more than a few minutes. Our neighbors had just installed an in-ground pool and hadn't yet put up a fence.

My neighbor heard something and looked out his upstairs bedroom window. Our toddler was at the steps to his pool. Thank God our neighbor heard her. Melanie had wandered off so quickly and quietly that we hadn't yet missed her.

Melanie had no fear of water. I had taken her to early swimming classes, so she was familiar with water. But she certainly wouldn't have been able to save herself, had she fallen in. We were so fortunate that it was not her time to leave us.

O Holy Spirit, Enlighten Me

Not everyone is as fortunate as we were. When it happens to you, you realize how quickly something like this can happen. You learn not to judge.

Shortly thereafter, our neighbors erected a fence. They let us know we were welcome to use the pool. As I loved to swim, I think we became part of their family. I had always wanted a pool, but as Dick didn't swim, he could have cared less. Sometimes I feel we should not have been at their house as often as we were, but they always made us feel welcome and encouraged us to come back.

As I loved water almost as much as I loved tennis, I would begin to go swimming instead of playing tennis. And so my tennis years would dwindle.

My older girls were young ladies by now and working. They were growing up so fast. I was glad I still had another young one to enjoy. I loved being a mother. As I grew and learned to understand my children, I enjoyed each one even more than the one before.

Because of the circumstances under which Melanie was born, I felt certain she was a gift from God. I knew I was supposed to have her. Melanie never needed reprimanded. She was always so good. I felt fortunate to have such a good child. I never needed to worry about her. She would be that way her entire life.

My oldest daughter would finish high school soon. She would attend summer school in order to have enough credits to graduate in three years. When she wanted to do something, nothing was going to stop her. She was ready to get on with her life.

By this time, I had decided the only way to get along with my oldest child was to stop being her mother and just become a friend. Born with a mind of her own, Kris had never welcomed advice from anyone, especially me. She was going to do her own thing in her own time.

When in a couple years she decided she was getting married, her father and I weren't very happy about it. We didn't care for her choice of husbands. We thought he had a drinking and drug problem, but Kris wouldn't see it.

It was only one week until the wedding. Tina and I had planned a wedding shower for Kris at our house. While preparing for the shower, which would be the next day, we received a shocking phone call. Dick's mother had passed away unexpectedly.

The following week, instead of preparing for the wedding, we were getting ready for a funeral. Dick's mother would be buried in the dress she had purchased for the wedding. The death of his mother would send Dick into a mood that lasted for years. If I thought he had been unpleasant before, I would find it could get worse. His father had passed away before I knew Dick. I didn't know how he handled that time in his life.

When his family had to share his mother's small estate with her husband of a few years, Dick was livid. His mother had worked very hard all her life to raise seven children on her own. She was by no means well-to-do.

A few months after his mother's death, his stepfather, who was still living in his mother's house, fell down the basement steps at their home and passed away as well. His mother's small estate would now include his stepfather's children. It was all Dick could think and talk about. He was constantly in a foul mood. It was something of which he just could not let go.

After one short year of marriage, Kris realized she had made a mistake in her choice of husbands and got a divorce. Used to being on her own, she moved into an apartment after a brief stay with her father and me. Within months, she would soon fall in love with another tenant, Dan. She and Dan had been coworkers years earlier while in high school.

A few months later, Dan took her to Florida to meet his mother. Before they came home, I had the feeling they had gotten married. Kris was never one to confide in me, it was just something I felt. When they came home, my feelings proved to be correct. While visiting his mother, they had gotten married. It had been so sudden, but it would prove to be one of the best moves my daughter ever made. He would prove to be the perfect husband for my daughter. The second time around, she had chosen very wisely.

While our life had taken on a new direction, my sister Pat's life would also change, which unfortunately wouldn't be pleasant. Although I had always found it hard to get along with my sister, since her surgery, Pat had become hostile with most everyone.

I often wondered what her children might be going through. Living with their mother could not have been a pleasant experience. Although Pat's husband stood by her for years, he eventually decided he could no longer stay married to her. Many wouldn't understand his decision and criticized him, but our family would never speak harshly about her husband. People always gossip, but we knew he had done everything he could for her and saw to it she had what she needed. We knew he was a good person, but we all have our limits, and he had reached his. His marriage was definitely ruining his health. And with her husband out of the picture, it would put more of the responsibility of Pat's everyday care on our family. Although her children helped, they were young and couldn't be expected to handle all of their mother's needs.

By this time, my father was no longer working and spent most of his time sitting on his bed, leaning on his portable stand, breathing his oxygen, and watching television. Although Dad had emphysema, he continued to smoke and often would smoke with the oxygen at his nose. He was always quick to assure us this was safe. I think only he believed this.

His health has caused him to drink less, which made it easier for me to communicate with him. My feelings toward him were beginning to soften. I no longer hated him, but I didn't feel sorry for him either. As long as I could remember, Dad had not taken care of himself.

My mother was still working every day. I don't think she was looking forward to the day when she retired and would be trapped all day in their tiny house with her husband. My father continued to argue with her about most everything. Mom's hobby would be raising violets in the basement. It wasn't hurting a thing, but he would even complain about that.

At some point, he must have been upset about the number of clothes Mom had because she would no longer buy anything new to wear. It didn't matter if it were for a wedding, graduation, or holiday. She would not buy anything new. She didn't have that many clothes. Never in her life did she have an abundance of clothing. Again I would not be able to understand how or why she continued to live with him.

A lifetime of stress finally caught up with my mother. She never seemed to be feeling well anymore. Her illnesses were becoming more and more frequent and serious. She

O Holy Spirit, Enlighten Me

would be hospitalized for gall bladder surgery. Her next hospital stay would be because of a severe headache. Mom had a brain aneurism. Years after Pat's brain surgery, it was now Mom's turn to have a procedure.

Mom survived the surgery, only to have a stroke that night that left her paralyzed on her left side. She was unable to talk clearly and was partially paralyzed on her left side, but her speaking would eventually correct itself. In time, she regained enough movement to walk with a severe limp, but she never regained the use of her left arm. But Mom never complained. She took her disability in stride, but she would never be quite the same. She was so fragile.

Out of the blue, my father would receive a totally unexpected phone call from someone I am pretty certain he had not spent a lot of time thinking of in his lifetime, Nancy, the daughter he had abandoned when she was just a baby. Not long after the communication opened between the two of them, Nancy would come to visit her long-lost father.

When I first saw her, I thought she very much resembled my older sister. I felt badly for her since she had been abandoned, yet I thought she had no idea what life with her father would have been like. Nancy had the appearance of someone who had led a very rough life. She obviously didn't have a lot of money. I hate to say it, but I thought she looked as though she could have been into drugs, alcohol, or both. Believing this, I could not let myself get close to her. I liked her, but I already had all I could handle with our family. I didn't have the energy to give anyone else.

After a short visit, Nancy returned to Las Vegas. A few years later, she would once again visit. After the second visit,

I didn't know if she and my father stayed in touch. I assume they did, but I don't really know.

Feeling I needed a break, I took a job at a local computer store. I felt as though I usually caught on to things pretty quickly, but I found I couldn't concentrate. What I was doing just didn't seem important to me. So when my employer was just about finished with my training, I quit. I felt bad about my decision, but my heart just wasn't into the job. The money wasn't that important, and there were more significant things in my life. I wanted to be available for my family.

Mom and Dad seldom left their home. Neither was doing very well. I was worried about both of them. Unable to stay in her home, Pat had been moved to an apartment. She needed someone to live with her. Pat had reached a point where she was no longer able to function without assistance. She had written checks and paid her bills. That was fine, but she overlooked making the deposit. All the checks bounced. It was becoming apparent that Pat was no longer capable of living alone. Even though I knew my sister needed someone to look after her, I wasn't able to invite my sister to live at my home. I knew that would be disastrous for everyone.

Years earlier, I had our small family over for Thanksgiving dinner. The day had gone extremely well until after dinner when we collected in the rec room downstairs. Melanie was bouncing a small ball. She wasn't being noisy. She was quietly entertaining herself with the ball. I guess the bouncing of the ball on the carpet must have upset my sister. For some totally unknown reason, Pat screamed at Melanie. No one had ever spoken to Melanie in that tone. We never had to discipline her. She was always so good. I didn't say anything to Pat, but

O Holy Spirit, Enlighten Me

once again, I wouldn't be able to understand my older sister. Things between us would never go smoothly.

Now alone, Pat needed a roommate. Carol, my younger sister who had been living in California, had once again divorced. After trying to start a small business on her own in California, she found she could no longer financially survive in California. Much to her dismay, Carol was left with no alternative but to return home. Mom and Dad sent her the money to get home. Thus, our dilemma with Pat was solved, and Carol found a home.

Carol was not happy about returning. She hated it here. I am certain she did not want to live with Pat. I was just happy she was returning. It would be nice to have someone to share in caring for our family. Life had become so hectic. It had been years and years since anyone hadn't needed help with something. It seemed someone always had a doctor's appointment or was in the hospital. It was a constant rotation of who was the most ill. I was beginning to feel overwhelmed. It seemed everyone was falling apart on me.

While Carol was sharing the apartment with Pat, Pat said one evening that someone was looking in the window at her. She was on the second floor. No one could have been looking in the window. Since she had changed significantly in her looks, I am certain Pat saw her reflection and no longer recognized her own image. Pat was having a hard time separating reality and hallucinations. My older sister once again reached a point where she had to be hospitalized. Her condition was worsening. While in the hospital, it was sometimes necessary for Pat to be fed intravenously.

After a couple days on the intravenous feeding, I noticed that Pat's personality would change. She was pleasant and made sense when she was talking. This had happened several times. If I had noticed this, did her doctors? I believed Pat had serious vitamin and mineral deficiencies, which were being corrected when she was fed intravenously but not when she relied on regular meals.

Meanwhile my father was often upset with the number of doctor appointments my mother had. He would make cruel comments to Mom. He felt the doctors were just after money and running unnecessary tests. It was my understanding that my father, in not too pleasant terms, expressed his feelings to the doctors. He was never one to keep his opinions to himself.

Unfortunately Pat had the same doctors. Although the doctors didn't drop my mother as a patient, they withdrew from Pat's case, leaving my sister without a doctor. Pat was now in the hospital without a regular doctor to look after her needs. She was in the hands of whichever intern was on call at the time.

On one icy winter night, I had driven Pat's two children to the hospital to visit with her. Soon after I entered the room, she snapped at me, telling me not to touch her. I withdrew from her bedside. I knew she didn't feel well, and if she felt up to visiting with anyone, it would have been her children.

This would be the last time I saw my sister. Shortly thereafter, early in the morning without any family present, Pat would pass away. Since the hospital did not really know what caused her death, an autopsy was performed. Weeks later, my mother told me that Pat had died of an accidental, intern-administered drug overdose.

Chapter 6

The summer after Pat passed away, Dick and I would begin traveling with our youngest daughter. Melanie had proved to be very athletic. She was only ten years old when she was invited to play on a softball team with girls older than herself.

And this would only be the beginning. Every summer through high school, we would be traveling with our daughter while she played softball. Melanie was fortunate to be playing with teams who would usually qualify for large tournaments at the end of the season, which would require traveling outside our local area. For me, this meant a vacation.

Traveling with Melanie and her teammates would be the first vacations I would ever enjoy. In addition to the trips within our home state, we would visit Oklahoma, Texas, Alabama, and North Carolina. There was never time to sightsee. Seventy-five percent of our time was spent watching softball games.

I. M. Free

For years, my life had pretty much consisted of taking someone to an appointment or running after something someone needed. It was nice to be with someone who was not ill. It was relaxing to get out of my routine and be around others. We would meet a lot of very nice people during this time. It was something positive to think about, which I very much needed. It was also something that helped me to keep my sanity.

Because of the visions I had experienced years earlier, I was now a firm believer in reincarnation. To me, this only made sense. I believe we are born over and over again. Each lifetime we learn a new lesson, and ultimately our soul becomes worthy of entering heaven. With all of our earthly faults, if each of us went to heaven when we died, wouldn't heaven soon become just like earth?

Within one year after her second marriage, Kris became pregnant. I believed perhaps the baby she was carrying was my older sister's soul. Although not positive, this would be something I felt very strongly. It had been a year and half since Pat had passed away.

It was the day before Thanksgiving. I had been cleaning and preparing for the dinner we would be having at our house the next day. Dick's family was going to be here. We were expecting about fifty people. Each family was going to bring a dish, so I didn't have to prepare a lot of things. It was just a matter of getting organized. I was never one to wait until the last minute to do things. I'm usually prepared for the unexpected. I was finished and ready to relax for the evening.

The phone rang. It was my mother. She felt she needed to go to the hospital. She just didn't feel right. I picked her up, and we headed to the emergency room. After examining her, they couldn't find any problem and were prepared to send her out the door. But suddenly everything went crazy. Mom was rushed back into the emergency room. At night's end, she was on life support. I was at the hospital until very late that evening. The next morning, I let my sister and brother tend to my mother. I needed to be home, at least for part of the day. I would see my mother that night.

At the hospital, my mother kept unhooking her tubes. It became necessary to tie down her arms. When I saw her that evening, she looked so uncomfortable. She wasn't able to speak; nor was she capable of writing legibly. But she obviously was not happy about her condition.

After a few days, believing my mother would not survive without life support, the doctors needed permission to disconnect her. My father would have to make this decision. But days passed, and he was having a terrible time struggling with that choice. He wasn't handling the situation very well. He looked tired and exhausted, but he would eventually sign the necessary papers.

After Pat's passing, Carol had moved into an apartment next door to our parents. When Carol stopped in after work, she found Dad passed out on the floor. Dad must have had a premonition because he had instructed Carol that under no circumstances were she to call an ambulance for him. Shocked at his condition, Carol forgot what he had told her and immediately called for the paramedics.

Dad was taken to the hospital and placed in intensive care. My mother had now been taken off life support and survived. Both would be in intensive care. And when it was time for my parents to be released from the intensive care unit to a step-down room, I stopped by the nurse's desk and left a message. I told them, "They don't get along. Please don't put them into the same room." I then left for the day.

The next morning I would find my request had been ignored. They put my parents into the same room, and as usual, they got into an argument. Neither was very strong. Still they could find the energy to exchange hostilities.

After words with my mother, my father was angry and decided he was leaving the hospital. When he didn't have any clothes and the staff wouldn't provide them, he was going to leave without the clothes. Of course the hospital staff was not going to let that happen. My father was admitted to the psychiatric ward. Had they known my father was used to getting his own way, they would have known treating him in this manner was not going to end well.

For years, my father had spent most of his time in an upright position. It enabled him to breathe with less effort. The last time I saw my father, he was constrained and unable to speak clearly. Did he have a stroke, or was he drugged? I had no idea what was going on with my father.

Shortly thereafter, my dad passed away in the psychiatric ward, somewhere I truly believe he did not belong. My father always had a short fuse, and while it was not easy for me to get along with him, I didn't for one second think he was in a state of mind that required being locked in a psychiatric ward. Just as when Pat had passed away, just too many things were happening too quickly. There wasn't time to ask questions. There was always something or someone else who needed my attention.

Weeks earlier, on Thanksgiving Day, we had been prepared to lose our mother. Instead it was one week before Christmas, and we were burying our father. And once my

O Holy Spirit, Enlighten Me

father passed away, my mother never once spoke about him. She didn't even want to hear anything about his funeral. After all these years of abuse, my mother was emotionally finished with my father.

Strangely, the summer before my father passed away, he and I were talking. Kris was pregnant for the second time.

I mentioned to my father, "I think you are going to be reborn to Kris."

My father looked at me and gave me the most pleasant smile I think he had ever given me in his life.

The spring after my father passed away, Kris would give birth to a baby boy on Good Friday. I truly felt this was a message from God.

When Mom left the hospital, she went to a nursing home. When they felt perhaps she could leave, we tried everything. She stayed at my house for a short time. I was not qualified to handle Mom's needs. We hired someone to come into her house to assist her. We bought an intercom so my sister, who was next door, would know if she needed something.

But nothing worked. Mom needed more intensive care than could be provided at home, and once again, she would go back to the nursing home. I believe my mother was sent from the hospital, home, or nursing home seven times in the past year. She was apparently never going to lead a self-sufficient life again. She was always going to need assistance.

With Dad gone and Mom never being able to live in her home again, I was left with the job of disposing of their home and its contents. Since they were heavy smokers, most everything in their home was unusable. My sister and brother smoked, so they took what they wanted. The rest was mostly thrown away. After clearing out the house, I cleaned it as well as I could. I could never get rid of the smoke smell. I listed the house for sale. Their house qualified for a government-assisted loan for the purchaser.

Not knowing how the system worked, I listed with a realtor. Unknown to me, once I had signed the papers, a licensed professional needed to make all future repairs to the home. Although my husband and I had built three homes and my brother's occupation was repairing and remodeling homes, we had to pay someone to make all necessary changes or repairs.

This was my first stupid mistake. I then replaced the smelly carpet and added new wallpaper to the bath and kitchen areas of the house. It was a small house, so it didn't require a large amount of carpet or wallpaper, but it was still a foolish thing for me to do after I had already listed the house.

In addition to the extra burden of disposing of their home and its contents, I had a two-inch-high pile of doctor and hospital bills that required my attention. Besides Medicare, Mom and Dad each had insurance with a different company. At that time, the healthcare system wasn't streamlined as it is today. It was necessary to make copies of everything, send each bill to the correct insurance company, and pay the correct amount. It was very confusing and time consuming.

After numerous roommates, my mother would share her room with a woman we all adored. She too would become a part of our family. When we visited our mother, all of us visited. I was glad Mom had a friend with whom she could spend the long days.

We had been called to the nursing home several times lately. Mom wasn't doing very well. Late one evening, I received a phone call from the nursing home. This time they wanted me to keep my mother company because her roommate had passed away. I stayed that evening until I felt comfortable about leaving. When I left my mother, I mentioned to her that Kris, the babies, and I would be in the next day to visit.

That night, as I talked to God about the day's events, I realized for the past year that my mother no longer wanted to be here. She had told me that. I realized I was the one holding my mother here. She was ready to leave, but I hadn't been ready to let her go. I said to God, "I don't want to see my mother suffer anymore."

The next day, about noon, Kris, her two children, and I entered my mother's room. Mom was lying in her bed and looked at us as we entered.

I said hi to her and then said to Courtney, "Come see Grandma."

As I reached for Courtney, my mother immediately shook her head no. She didn't say anything. She just closed her eyes, and she was gone. She knew we were coming, and I know she waited for us to get there.

Although each had been sick for a very long time, in four short years, I had lost half of my childhood family. To say the least, I was exhausted. It had been years since I felt as though I could sit down and actually relax. It had been a long road, lasting many years, and now it was over.

My mother had filled so much of my time over the years that I considered her my best friend. I had lost contact with my school friends, the girls with whom I had worked, and my tennis buddies. At least my sister Carol was here. Carol would now become my closest friend and confidant.

Chapter 7

I would recall a conversation I had with my mother years earlier. We were discussing my new relationship with God. I wished I could make my mother understand the peace that could come with communicating with God.

At the time, my mother informed me that she didn't believe in God. She told me, "I am an atheist. Life on earth is hell." Although my mother hadn't been to church for many years, she had been brought up in the Catholic faith. I was surprised to hear she didn't believe in God. By this time, I too believed life on earth was hell, but at the same time, I also believed life on earth could be heaven. I believe it all depended upon where we were in our spiritual growth.

It seemed everyone in my family was going through some sort of despair. Other than the anguish I felt for them, my life hadn't been that bad. I felt I had been very fortunate. Most of all, I had my health, which I thank God for all the time. At the time, I truly believed the bad years were behind me. I was looking forward to life without stress. But that would prove to be a fantasy. The peace I had hoped would fill my life after the deaths of my sister and parents just wasn't about to happen.

I would try several different jobs. I wasn't content with any of them and didn't stick with it for very long. I felt I needed a refresher course. Computers were now the way to do things. I was taking adult training classes so I might freshen up my typing and accounting skills. I was at the class when I received an emergency phone call.

My husband had a doctor's appointment, which ended up with him going immediately to the hospital. At the hospital, it was decided he needed emergency heart surgery. They felt he should go to a larger hospital about an hour away. Thus, that same night, he was transferred to the bigger facility. They would do the surgery first thing the next morning.

At the hospital, they had hoped that stents would be sufficient to clear the blockages he had in his arteries. But after hours of surgery and not seeing the desired results, he would go directly into open heart surgery. It would be more than twelve hours before we were notified they had finished his surgery.

Prior to his operation, Dick had been working out of the area and had been gone all week. He was sleeping on a garage floor in the southern part of the state. He had changed employers and was earning half what he previously brought home. Although we didn't have a mortgage, we still had utilities, groceries, taxes, insurance, and so on. And because Dick never had any responsibility handling our household expenses, he had no idea what amount was needed to just make ends meet. Had I not gone back to work, we would not have been able to pay our bills. I had asked him to change jobs, but he ignored me. He was going to do what he wanted to do.

Dick had been carrying his anger about his mother's estate for quite a long time. It had been years since we last moved, but he was still resentful toward me about it. He could really carry a grudge. I truly believe this combination of events was why he had a problem. Your blood doesn't flow as it should when you are constantly carrying anger in your body. It just isn't healthy. After surgery, Dick was going to be off work for some time. He needed time to think about life, and this would be a good time for him to do it.

While Dick had his problems with his health, my middle daughter was also having issues. Tina had been displaying some erratic behavior for some time. I didn't understand. Perhaps all the family stress was getting to her as well. Tina had always been a very sensitive girl.

The first time I noticed she was behaving differently, she had been living with her high school sweetheart, to whom she was engaged. When that relationship didn't work out, she had moved home. It was then I really noticed how much she had changed. As time passed, she would have periods when she seemed perfectly normal. Then suddenly she would say or do something that made no sense. We were concerned, but no one specific event said she definitely had a problem.

When Tina met someone and fell in love for the second time, she once again became engaged. I am certain she never cared about anyone as much as she cared for John. She was crazy about him. Unfortunately in time, this relationship also would end.

After the second breakup, I believe Tina was depressed for quite some time. Something was happening to her. As

O Holy Spirit, Enlighten Me

the years passed, it was becoming increasingly harder to understand what was going on in her mind.

Tina had a warm and loving personality. She would make a good impression when she applied for a job. But once she had the job, the stress of working regular hours and the responsibility of the position would take its toll. She would mentally lose control of her life and end up getting fired. It was happening over and over again.

Although we were aware something was wrong with Tina, as she was now considered an adult, we didn't know what to do or how to go about getting her help. When I tried to talk with her about seeing someone, she wasn't going to have anything to do with that.

I had never had any problem getting along with Tina. She had always been a pleasant daughter. We had always been close, but to her, I had become her enemy, and I had no idea why. In her mind, I was the one who needed to see a doctor. There was nothing wrong with her.

On one occasion, she accused me of spilling a drink in her car. I had no idea what she could be talking about. I hadn't been near her car. Next, she accused me of sticking pins into a voodoo doll, causing her pain. This made absolutely no sense to me. I had never heard of such a thing. Where did these thoughts come from? Was it from the strange movies she watched while living with her first boyfriend? I had no idea. Her life was getting more and more bizarre. Eventually Tina would physically attack me, stating she wanted to kill me. I was at a loss. I had no idea what was going on in her mind. Somehow in Tina's thinking, I was behind all of her problems.

When Tina's current boss called me concerning Tina, he said he felt bad, but he had to let her go. Tina believed someone was sending messages to her through her computer. He felt she needed to see someone.

When I couldn't convince Tina she needed help, she went to visit her older sister. She was confused and making no sense whatsoever at the time. Somehow Kris convinced her to go with her to talk with a minister. And as the minister talked with Tina, he suggested she be taken to the crisis center. Surprisingly Tina agreed to go.

The visit to the crisis center ended up with Tina being admitted to a behavioral hospital. After a few days, she was diagnosed as paranoid schizophrenic. After Tina left the hospital, she had a caseworker who contacted her regularly to see if she were taking her medication and doing okay. Tina would forever declare she didn't need medicine. The medication helped somewhat, but by no means cured her.

Even though we now had a diagnosis, I really couldn't understand what was happening to my beautiful daughter. I knew nothing about schizophrenia. Unable to understand Tina's illness, most of her friends had disappeared. She was becoming increasingly isolated from the real world.

Melanie was in the final year of high school when she went to see an orthodontist about the slight overlap of her upper front teeth. Believing it shouldn't be too much of a problem to correct, the orthodontist said he could correct her bite in one year. That sounded reasonable, so we made arrangements to have the braces applied. What could possibly go wrong?

As we neared the end of the year, I received a letter from the orthodontist. When I read it, I was never more upset with

O Holy Spirit, Enlighten Me

anyone in my life. I could not believe what I was reading. He stated Melanie was going to have a problem with her jaw. He recommended she have surgery to break her jaw and reset it. I thought, *you have got to be kidding. Break my daughter's jaw and reset it? Why?* I was so angry that I could not even talk to the orthodontist. I didn't ever want to set eyes on him again.

Melanie had no problem with her jaw before he worked on her teeth. Now I was supposed to go along with letting someone break my daughter's jaw and reset it. I just couldn't let go of my anger and total disgust with this orthodontist. I had never contacted a lawyer before in my life. I didn't think I would ever consider suing anyone. But this time, I could not accept what he had done to my daughter.

I contacted several lawyers, all to no avail. Even though all I wanted was my money returned, no one would even consider representing me. One lawyer stated he wouldn't take a case that represented less than $50,000.

Having already paid for what was supposed to be an easy fix, I only wanted someone else to correct my daughter's bite, and I certainly didn't think I should have to be the one to pay for it. Although I never repeated anything derogatory to anyone about the dentist, I had sent a letter to the local paper regarding my predicament. The letter was printed. I didn't name the orthodontist.

Shortly thereafter, I received a letter from a lawyer representing the orthodontist. The lawyer stated I was defaming the orthodontist and he was considering suing me. What a joke! No one would represent me, but he had no problem finding someone to represent him.

I sent a copy of the orthodontist's letter to the lawyer. I asked him, "Would you let him work on your children's teeth?" I also stated he should tell the orthodontist to sue me. I told him, "I want to be heard. I haven't said anything that isn't true, and the first thing I will do is call the local paper and tell them he is suing me."

I never heard from the lawyer again. After contacting numerous people regarding my complaint, after nearly one year, I realized I was fighting a losing battle. No one was going to help me. Melanie would eventually see another orthodontist, have two teeth pulled, and once again endure another year of braces. Just as suspected, it was not necessary to break her jaw.

It would take me years to forgive that orthodontist, but in time, I realized he was human and had made a huge error in judgment. I let go of my anger.

Chapter 8

After both of our parents were gone, as much as my sister hating living in our hometown, Carol decided to purchase a duplex near the hospital, a very nice place with the upstairs being the second apartment. She felt the extra income would help her make the payments. She had moved in and was getting her life organized.

At the same time I was upset with Melanie's orthodontist, Carol had a routine dental cleaning. A smoker, she was having problems with her gums. The day after the cleaning, she became terribly ill. One day she was perfectly healthy; the next she was terribly ill. Days went by, and she wasn't getting any better. It had come on so quickly.

It became necessary for her to see a doctor. Upon seeing him, Carol would be told her kidneys were no longer functioning and she would need a kidney transplant. Without a new kidney, she would need dialysis to cleanse her body.

Knowing Carol needed a transplant, I felt I should offer one of mine. My body had not yet accepted the deaths of my sister and my parents. I was also terribly concerned about Tina. I just felt I couldn't risk having a problem with my own health right now. Feeling I needed more time, I told Carol, "Give me some time. I will do it, but I have to get my own life back in a good place. Right now I am too exhausted." Carol told me she didn't want me to give up a kidney. She knew I was already dealing with a lot.

In an effort to get her onto a transplant list, we would go to two of the largest hospitals in the state to see about putting Carol on that list. Upon talking with doctors at each hospital, one facility would not put her on the list because she didn't have a method of paying for the medication she would need for the rest of her life after the transplant. The other would not put her on the list because she continued to smoke.

A doctor she spoke with at one of the hospitals informed her that a virus had entered her body. This particular virus had attacked the kidneys and lungs. We knew exactly when she had become ill and when and where the virus had probably entered her body. Even with this knowledge, Carol said nothing to the dentist who had cleaned her teeth. She accepted her fate.

Even though the local hospital was only one block from Carol's home, she chose to do her dialysis at home. Independent as always, she was determined to do it herself. She had only been on dialysis a short time when she became very ill and had to be hospitalized. This time she was diagnosed with peritonitis.

Carol shared her apartment with two cats. Foolishly, she would let the cats on the bed as she was doing the dialysis. Infection, most probably from her cats, had entered her body.

When she went home from the hospital, she knew she needed to be more careful with her dialysis.

Still living at home, Tina needed to have her own space. She liked to cook and was a good housekeeper. She usually kept things pretty clean and organized. When Tina stayed on her medication, she was quite capable of taking care of herself. The problem was that she would never accept she needed the medication and would often stop taking it.

Tina was no longer able to work forty hours a week. She qualified for housing assistance. Much to my surprise, Carol offered her upstairs apartment to Tina. I was thrilled. It hadn't even entered my mind. I wouldn't have been comfortable letting Tina move just anywhere, but I was at ease with the idea of Carol being downstairs. She could keep an eye on Tina.

I was surprised when Tina accepted Carol's offer, and she soon moved into the upstairs apartment. Although it was a relief for me at home, I still couldn't stop worrying about Tina, who was always on my mind.

In time, Carol had become too weak to continue working and would find it necessary to go onto disability. Carol always had so much pride. She enjoyed working and being around people. Disability could not have been an easy thing for her to accept. No longer able to work, Carol found it hard to survive on her small disability check. The meager amount of money she had in the bank was too much for her to qualify for food assistance.

Believing it would allow her to qualify for assistance if she spent some of her savings, she purchased a few things for her home. Next, she found the rent she received from Tina was considered income. She still didn't qualify for assistance.

What was she supposed to do? She needed the rental income to make her house payment.

Unable to work, Carol was now home most of the time. Even though Tina was upstairs, Carol could hear her. Tina talked to the voices she constantly heard in her head. So often, when I would hear or see Tina doing this, it would break my heart. I so wished I could do more for her.

Unfortunately, in a very short time, I think Carol found living with Tina as stressful as I did. With all her disappointments, she really didn't need this. Carol couldn't get any assistance, make ends meet, or work, and because she hadn't quit smoking, she didn't qualify for a transplant. Nothing was going her way. How much disappointment could a person take?

Years earlier, Carol had moved to California without a job and about a hundred dollars. I would never have done something like that. She married while still in high school, something else I would never have done. Carol and I had always been so different. I would wonder, "How is she coping with all of this?" I was certain I couldn't deal with all of that stress and disappointment. Outwardly, she seemed to be coping. Carol didn't offer any clues as to how she felt.

I was working two jobs at the time, but neither were full time. I was doing office work at home for a local company, and I was also working for a moving company. Except for my experience with the custard stand and now the moving company, I had never done anything except office work. I decided I really didn't like to do office work. I quit the job I did at home.

I enjoyed the work I did for the moving company. We would go into people's homes and pack their belongings prior to their moving. I don't know if I liked the work or my coworkers. The women were good company, and we could talk while we worked, something one can't do very easily when doing office work. I found it relaxing.

After a full day of work, I would feel I needed to check on Carol and Tina every evening. I couldn't stop worrying about them until I had checked on their well-being. Carol did not like I felt the need to check on her continually. Still even knowing this, I couldn't stop myself.

Carol had been dealing with her kidney failure for less than two years when she once again became ill and had to be hospitalized. She was diagnosed with peritonitis for the second time. This time, it was much more serious than before. She was extremely ill and in unbearable pain.

This time, Carol would not leave the hospital. My brother and his girlfriend were with her when she passed away. When my brother called with the news, I could not believe she was gone. I think I was in a state of shock. For years, I had felt something before it would happen. I hadn't felt this coming. I knew the others were going to pass away, but I didn't expect this. I felt God had abandoned me. I was angry at Him. How could He do this?

Chapter 9

A few days after Carol passed away, we would have a small funeral for her. Tina wouldn't go to the service. She was in a world of her own. I had no idea what was going on in her mind. She didn't volunteer anything.

Carol had no will of any sort. The house would be left empty. We had no claim on it. Carol had no other relatives. My brother and nephews would remove her belongings. Tina would stay in the upstairs apartment a few weeks longer while we worked to make arrangements for her to move. I wanted Tina to live somewhere close to me so I could continue to check on her. We found a very nice apartment about one mile from home. As soon as we could, we moved Tina into her new residence.

I had quit talking to God on a regular basis after Carol passed. My faith had taken a blow. I felt lost. After feeling so close to God for so many years, I had closed my mind to Him as well. I didn't reach out to my friends. I didn't want to share anything with them, and I had nothing left to give them. With Carol gone, I didn't feel close to anyone.

When my family members had been sick, I would go for drives by myself. I wished I had a place I could go and just scream to release the emotions I was feeling. It had been so hard to watch them hurting and not being able to do anything to make their lives better.

It wasn't until after my younger sister was gone that I realized how much and how long I had been pushing myself. I had been running constantly for years. I no longer remembered what it was to sit down and not have something that needed my attention. I was unable to relax. I had witnessed my family endure so much pain for as long as I could remember. My mind was so full of pain. I knew I needed to get it out of my body. Carrying the extra baggage couldn't be healthy.

When I wasn't with Tina or my job, I would spend my spare time writing about my experiences with my family. This was my way of releasing my emotions. There had been so many disappointments over the years. They had endured so much, but to their credit, none of them had spent their time complaining about their illnesses.

As I wrote, I realized God had warned me of what was to come. He had cautioned me at least two times. But believing He couldn't possibly take anyone else from me, I had overlooked His messages. Unknowingly, because of the pain I felt from the loss of my other sister and my parents, with my mind closed, the messages had gone right past me.

Other than the time I spent working, writing, or staying with Tina, my only outlet was attending Melanie's college basketball games. She had received an athletic scholarship to a local college, and she was on the varsity basketball team.

Melanie had also been asked to join the softball team, but she declined. She had played enough softball in high school. She no longer enjoyed it as she once had. She focused on her basketball instead.

While talking with a parent of one of Melanie's teammates, she asked if I would like to drive for their company. They offered a service much like a taxi. For example, they would offer rides to doctor appointments for the elderly. She set up an appointment for me with one of the other drivers. I rode with the lady as she picked up one elderly person after another, assisting them when necessary.

As I watched her help the elderly patients, my mind wandered to the many times I had done the same thing with my mother. The vivid memory was upsetting. She drove past my sister's now-empty house. It had been nearly two years since Carol passed away. I hadn't been near her home since we moved out Tina's belongings. This also upset me.

I began talking to the lady as she drove. I told her things I had not said to anyone in the years since Carol's passing. I was like a motor mouth. I couldn't stop talking about the things that hurt inside of me. Just like Tina, I had become isolated and hardly recognized myself. I knew I needed to get over mourning my family and join the world again.

I had spent hours writing. When I finished releasing all my hurt into those pages, I had nearly 150 pages of hurt, pain, and disappointment. But I was beginning to feel better about things. I was beginning to let go of the past.

After some time, believing I had an additional copy of my writing on my computer, I threw all those memories into the trash. I didn't ever want to relive that portion of my life. Years later, I discovered that I didn't have a copy of my writings. When I realized that segment of my life was gone forever, I thanked God I had thrown away those pages. Even now, years later, I can't and don't want to remember many of the things that happened in those years.

In the beginning, I had enjoyed my job with the moving company, but the working conditions kept changing. They were asking us to do more and more work with less help. When they scheduled a huge job involving a farmer who was moving south, they needed extra help. I had suggested that perhaps Tina could occasionally work with us. I knew Tina could never work more than one day at a time and explained that to them. Over the years, I had learned Tina's capacity for working. When she was tired, the voices in her head would take over, and she would be almost useless. She just could not function.

This particular day, Tina was with me. I had driven to the job thirty to forty miles from home. As I worked, one of the ladies came and told me Tina had left. Unable to cope with the environment, Tina had walked down the road. She could not have had any idea where she was going. Thank God I had driven to the job. I caught up with her and took her home.

Soon after that experience, I was expected to follow one of the men to a job. I had never driven the box truck. I always let one of the other ladies drive the truck to the job, but this morning I was alone. It was now eight in the morning, and I was driving through a construction zone with multiple lanes of traffic in an area of a city of which I was not familiar. And to top it all off, it was raining. I know my limitations, and I had no business driving that truck. I was not happy. They were putting my life and perhaps the life of someone else in jeopardy. No longer happy with my job, when the company decided to move their packing division to another city, I decided it was time to quit.

Over the years, Tina's condition continued to decline. Since I was no longer working, I would begin spending time with her every day. We would either go to breakfast or lunch.

Melanie's college basketball team had a tremendous year. They qualified for the national tournament, and were the last team to be invited to play in the tourney. We joined several parents of Melanie's teammates and attended.

While attending, a small group of us would take time each day and visit the Queen of Peace statue, a thirty-foot-high sculpture of the Virgin Mary. It is a beautiful piece of work. We were told, if we were to rub her feet, it would bring us luck. Each day, we would return to the statue and rub her feet. Although we can't take all of the credit, our efforts must not have gone unnoticed. The girls won the tournament. They were the number-one team in their division that year.

Unable to keep a job for any length of time, Tina had gone on full disability. Working for even a short period of time would prove to be too much for her. Still firmly believing that nothing was wrong with her, Tina continued having trouble staying on her medication. When she wasn't taking her pills, she would be unable to function. She couldn't carry on a conversation without someone having to repeat himself or herself over and over again. She could never accept she needed her medication.

Years earlier, while still working, Tina had purchased a beautiful brown cocker spaniel who had been her companion for years. Once again, Tina was not taking her medication. When not on her pills, the voices would take over Tina's life. She would become obsessed with cleansing her body. Although she wouldn't take her medicine, she would consume multiple kinds of vitamins.

While in this state of mind, Tina began giving her dog vinegar water to drink. She was going to cleanse the dog as well. Of course, the dog wouldn't drink the foul-tasting water. Tina would put bowl cleaner into her toilet and not flush it. The dog would drink that water. I repeatedly asked her not to do this. In Tina's compromised state of mind, she couldn't understand what she was doing to her dog. Eventually Tina's beautiful dog hemorrhaged and died. Fortunately Tina would never understand what she had done to her dog.

On another occasion, she began spray-painting the apartment complex where she lived. She would spray-paint anything she felt needed freshening up. She went too far when she spray-painted the community mailboxes, which are federal property. You do not paint federal property. Her mental illness was the only thing that kept her from being charged.

Once Tina quit taking her medication, I could never get her to start taking it again. The voices would tell her not to take it, convincing her she didn't need it. At those times, the voices controlled Tina's life. The only way to get Tina back onto her medication would be when she was hospitalized. They would force her to take it.

Tina had been off her medication for quite some time. I was very concerned about her. She could no longer keep track of her bills. She was using a credit card to pay for pop and cigarettes. In addition to the cost of her purchases, there was a ten-dollar fee every time she used the card.

Years earlier, before being diagnosed as schizophrenic, Tina had gone bankrupt. She had only recently qualified for a credit card, and the cards she received were the worst ones out there. Her life was getting totally out of control. Concerned and unable to get Tina to begin taking her medicine, I visited the crisis center, asking for assistance. Unable to get anywhere constructive, I had left the crisis center and returned home.

I just entered the door at home when the phone rang. It was the crisis center. The girl said to me, "You are not going to believe this."

While I had been at the crisis center asking for help, Tina had gone to the police station and asked for help. She told them she was afraid of the voices. The police had taken her to the crisis center. Although not at all happy about the decision that was made for her, she was once again hospitalized and forced to take her medication.

Chapter 10

Tina had recently connected with a fellow she knew from high school, Kelly, and they had begun to keep in touch. Since I had been with Tina when she first ran into Kelly at a local gas station, I knew her new friend was a few years older than her. He seemed like a very nice person.

Melanie would graduate college soon. She would be the first member of our family to get a college degree. I was proud of her, as she had pretty much put herself through college with working and scholarships.

After Carol passed away, I had kept her ashes. Melanie suggested that both of us take a trip to California, back to where Carol was happiest, after her graduation. We were making arrangements to leave town. But before Melanie and I left for our trip, she and I paid a visit to Kelly. I wanted him to know what he was getting into with Tina. When I explained Tina's illness to Kelly, he understood. Kelly explained he had an uncle who was schizophrenic. No one with whom I communicated was familiar with schizophrenia. I felt it was destiny that Kelly came into our lives when he did.

Knowing how lonely Tina was, we asked Kelly to keep in touch with Tina while we were gone. He said he would. It was always really hard for me to leave Tina. I knew she was a grown adult, but much of her was still childlike. She was totally incapable of making sound judgments about things. She kept me on my toes, trying to keep her on an even keel. I knew I would worry about her and what she might do the entire time I was gone.

Before I left town, I wanted to let my neighbor know we would be out of town for a short while. Frieda had always followed Melanie's accomplishments. Frieda and I had one thing in common. In nearly the same time span as I had lost my sister, father, and mother, Frieda had lost her husband, mother, and son, her only child. Feeling her loss was even greater than mine kept me from feeling sorry for myself. Knowing she was usually alone, we had gotten into the habit of asking Frieda to join us for holidays and special occasions.

I usually spoke with Frieda on the phone. She would come to our house. I hadn't been inside her home for years. I went to her place to say good-bye. Once inside, I couldn't believe the disarray. It obviously hadn't been cleaned in many months. It suddenly became apparent she wasn't really doing well. The car was packed, and we were ready to leave. Feeling I should do something, I realized I could not do anything for her except run to the store for the food she requested.

Later that day, Melanie and I left. We drove until we needed gas. As I got out of the car to fill the tank, the music on the gas station speakers immediately got my attention. The

O Holy Spirit, Enlighten Me

song was "Babe." The words are, "I'm leaving. I must be on my way."

I got chills when I heard the song. I knew God was telling me something. As I often did, I went through a list of family members in my mind. When I hit the right person, I would usually feel it. I went through the entire family, and nothing hit. I didn't know for what I was being prepared.

I didn't have to wait long. When I called home the next day, I was greeted with the news that Frieda had passed away. Kris had come home for something. Someone knocked at the door, inquiring about Frieda. This person was concerned when he had gone to her door and didn't receive any response. Trying to help, Kris entered the house. She found Frieda. She had passed away. I was totally unprepared for this news. This was not the way to start a cross-country trip. Tina and Frieda would remain in my mind the entire time.

While we were gone, I would call Tina daily. After a few days, just as I had feared, Tina was losing touch with reality. What could I do? I was halfway across the country.

We drove each day until we were tired and stopped when it felt like it was the thing to do. When we reached California, we stayed with my aunt for a couple days. While there, we drove Carol's ashes to Mission Bay and released them. Carol had spent some of her happiest years at Mission Bay. Knowing how much Carol hated our hometown, I felt this was where she preferred to be.

We had driven across the center of the United States while going to California. We would return via the northern route. We saw so many national landmarks in such a short period of time. The only time we might have made a poor choice was when we decided to drive through the mountains in Wyoming and hadn't paid attention to the fact there were snowstorm warnings for the day.

I was still a naïve traveler. We were only partially up the mountain when the snow began. In a matter of minutes, a foot of snow was covering the road. Many places didn't have guardrails. We could no longer see the road. Then unbelievably, a snowplow made a U-turn right in front of us. While many people were stranded, we followed the snowplow out of the mountain.

As we entered Yellowstone National Park, no sooner did we drive up to Old Faithful before the geyser went off.

The entire trip was perfect. I repeatedly said, "Frieda and Carol are with us."

On the way through Iowa, we once again visited the Virgin Mary statue where we had been for Melanie's tournament. They had now also built a thirty-five-foot stainless steel monument of Jesus. It was beautiful the first time I saw it, and it was even lovelier now.

When I next spoke with Tina, I knew we needed to get home as soon as possible. Her birthday was in a few days. I knew she would be very disappointed if we were not home. That was the childlike part of Tina's personality. She would forever be sensitive about some things. So we would hurry the end of our trip in order to get home before her birthday. It was none too soon. Tina was getting worse every day.

Once Melanie and I had introduced ourselves to Kelly, he too had become a new member of our family. He was the best thing that ever happened to Tina or me. In the years to come, I appreciated all the things he did for my daughter. No matter what she needed him to do, he was always there for her and never let her down. Sometimes I would feel I just couldn't go on. I was so drained from dealing with Tina's ups and downs. It was then Kelly would remind me, "She can't help it." It helped so much just having someone understand.

Kris and Melanie had their own lives to live. Tina was not their priority. Dick stayed as uninvolved as possible. When Tina once again maxed out her credit cards and could no longer make the minimum payments, the calls from the collection agencies would begin, which would upset Tina, causing her to withdraw even more. Stress always made her illness worse. Although the calls upset her, it was not enough to ever teach her to stop using the cards. I would discover she had several cards she had maxed out. Trying to lessen the stress, I foolishly paid off the balances for her, with the warning, "Do not do this again." Unknown to me, Tina would almost immediately open a new account somewhere else.

Realizing Tina's mental condition was slowly worsening, I became her legal guardian. Not ever wanting to accept she had a problem, I was surprised Tina agreed to sign the papers, allowing me to do this. Dick and I would put our personal possessions into a trust so we could name Melanie to be in control of Tina's portion. It was our hope, when Dick and I were no longer here to look after Tina, Melanie would look after her.

When the facility Tina visited for her doctor appointments and medication closed, she would once again stop taking her pills. I had no one from whom to request assistance. Once again the voices would take over Tina's life. She began throwing her personal possessions into the dumpster at her apartment complex. One thing after another was disappearing.

When I became aware of the type of things she was throwing away, I began going to her complex at night and checking the dumpster. I simply could not afford to replace all the necessities she was tossing away. She had thrown away many of her clothes. One evening a friend accompanied me. Beneath an old mattress, we found Tina's birth certificate, utility bills, medical papers, and other various papers. She had previously thrown away her driver's license, which we had to replace. I assumed she believed, if she threw away her identification, she was getting rid of the person who was constantly talking to her in her head. She was always telling me that person was not her.

She wasn't done. She disconnected her stove and refrigerator. She removed everything from her cupboards and closets and put them into the center of her living room. She upset the bedroom furniture. When I saw what she had done, instead of contacting the crisis center, as I should have done, I cleaned her apartment. The next day, she had done the same thing. This time, Kelly helped her put things back.

When I again called the crisis center, explaining what she had been up to, they weren't able to help me. They needed to see what she had done. With the closure of the mental facility, there were others with conditions worse than Tina, so they took priority. They didn't feel she was a danger to herself or anyone else.

Shortly thereafter, Tina got into an argument with the landlord. I knew it was time to get something done before she was thrown out of her apartment. It took some time, but Tina once again would eventually be hospitalized. When she left the hospital this time, she told me, "That is the last time I am going there."

Upon her release, Tina would now receive her medical needs from a new facility and doctor. This time I had someone with whom I could speak. I liked her new doctor. For the first time, I felt she was in good hands.

From the very beginning, I had always gone with Tina to each of her appointments. She protested each time she had to go. This was the only way I could be sure she kept her appointments. She still believed nothing was wrong with her and she didn't need to go to the doctor.

Kris and her family had moved to Louisiana years earlier. When Dick, Melanie, her husband of a few years, Lance, and I wanted to visit Kris in Louisiana, I asked Tina to join us. I would never be able to go and leave Tina alone without anyone in the family to contact.

As with her father, change always upset Tina. She did not want to go. But after much pleading and coaxing, Tina finally agreed to it. Concerned about Tina's ability to control herself on the plane, I visited her doctor and asked about changing her medication. I explained I feared Tina would lose control on the plane and get all of us kicked off. The doctor changed her medication, and Tina showed a definite improvement. It was slight, but it was working better than the medication she had been taking. I was so grateful.

We made the trip without any problems. Tina handled the time away from home surprisingly well. We had a really nice time, and I was so glad she went with us.

But just when I would think we had turned a corner, Tina would again refuse to take her medication. I visited her doctor, explaining to him, in her mind, she no longer needed medication and would no longer willingly take it. The doctor allowed me to fill her prescriptions, and Tina never knew I was spiking her drinks with her medication.

I would crush her pills, dissolve them, and add them to her drink when she was not looking. It was something of which I was not proud, but it was keeping her out of the hospital. This worked for nearly one year, but all good things must come to an end.

Someone from the facility who oversaw the prescriptions that patients were receiving called Tina. When Tina said she hadn't filled her prescriptions, the woman told her someone was. Tina called and asked, "Are you filling my prescriptions?" I told her I was. I explained to her, "I don't want to be around you if you aren't on your medication."

For the first time, she willingly started taking the medicine. She later stated the only reason she did was because I said I didn't want to be around her if she didn't. After all these years, why didn't I think of that sooner?

Chapter 11

Not long after I had paid off Tina's credit cards, I discovered she had once again maxed out new ones. I was terribly disappointed. This time I was not about to be foolish enough to pay them a second time. Instead I wrote to each creditor, explaining, if they had taken the time to check her credit rating, they would have known she shouldn't have qualified for a credit card. I stated she was mentally ill and lived on disability. The creditors graciously wrote off the balance to her accounts.

I felt perhaps stopping the phone calls regarding her unpaid balances would take the pressure off Tina. I was constantly trying to make my daughter's life as stress-free as possible. I knew Tina felt badly about what she had done, but she just couldn't stop herself. They sent the applications via mail. They made it easy for her to get a card, and she couldn't turn down the offer.

Having removed the tension from her life, due to phone calls about unpaid credit card balances, things seemed to go a little more smoothly. I believed she was really trying to improve her way of life. She would often feel down because her sisters had so much and she had nothing. She wanted to be married and have a family, as they did.

At these times, I would tell her, "Don't look at all the people who have more than you. Look at all the people who don't have as much as you do. Between your disability check and the assistance you receive, you don't have to worry about having a roof over your head. That is a lot more than many people have."

I would often wonder why some people have life so good and others struggle. In my heart, I believe we all have just what we are supposed to have. I believe my own life choices have been something I needed to do to free my soul from guilt I felt from my last life.

It is my belief I was my grandmother in my last life. When forced to choose between my children and my father, I left my children and went out West to look after my father. My daughter, my mother in this lifetime, had to pretty much raise her three brothers. In my previous life, I died in my early forties of stomach cancer. I believe my guilt and inability to make peace with myself brought on the cancer. And I believe this because I am basically the same person in this life. Except in this lifetime, I think I have my priorities, that is, my immediate family, straight.

I would awaken, and little by little, these things would be revealed to me. I know how hard this is for many to believe. It happened to me, and I cannot believe it occurred. Many won't believe my version of life, but I am 100 percent comfortable with my beliefs. And only God knows the truth.

O Holy Spirit, Enlighten Me

It was Wednesday, my seventy-second birthday. I picked up Tina, as usual, that morning. For years, she and I had visited the Goodwill stores in our area. Although I couldn't afford to buy Tina things at full price, the Goodwill stores were affordable. It would lift Tina's spirits to have something new to look at or wear.

We were going to K-Mart this morning instead of our usual visit to the Goodwill stores. Tina wasn't feeling well. She had been coughing a lot. She had been for months. Again that morning, I warned her she was going to be unable to breathe freely or go out in the cold, like my father and brother. She would just get frustrated at hearing the same old words.

At K-Mart, as I went and looked for what I needed, Tina stayed at the jewelry counter. When I returned, she had tried on a ring of emerald and diamonds, her birthstone. She begged me, "Could I please have this for my birthday this year?"

It was March. Her birthday wasn't until May. It was a pretty ring. I told her I would think about it and walked off. As I walked, I was asking my conscience, "Should I buy the ring?"

Years ago, I had gotten into the habit of asking my guiding voice about unnecessary purchases. It helped me to stay on my budget without worrying about having enough money next month to make ends meet. Surprisingly it felt like the right thing to do, and I bought Tina her birthstone ring.

We were going to Melanie and Lance's for dinner that evening. It was unusual for Mel to ask us to dinner, but since it was my birthday, I didn't think too much of it.

After finishing dinner, we were relaxing at the table. Melanie handed me a picture. As I looked at it, I realized it was a sonogram. I smiled. It was her way of telling me she was expecting. She and Lance were going to become parents. I was very pleased and pleasantly surprised. We hadn't had a baby in the family for so long. My other two grandchildren were now in their twenties and lived in Louisiana. Now I understood why I kept my high chair. I was going to need it.

Tina didn't say much. Once again, one of her sisters was going to enjoy something she never would. Although glad for Melanie's good fortune, I could feel the sadness it caused Tina. She wanted a husband, a nice home, and a family, but at forty-seven, it didn't seem likely to be in her future.

A day or so after Melanie's news, I could feel something was wrong. Often when someone close to me was troubled, I would be able to feel the unrest in my body. In my mind, I would start with one person and go through the family until I would know who was troubled about something. This morning I was experiencing that sort of feeling.

Tina and I were in the car, returning from our usual morning together. I was just about to drop off Tina at her apartment. I said to Tina, "Something is wrong. I can feel it."

Again I silently in my mind went through everyone's name, and when I said "Tina," I knew who was troubled. I looked at her as I told her I knew it was her. She didn't say anything. She didn't deny it; nor did she offer an explanation. I dropped her off and went home. I would find out soon enough what was troubling her. She wasn't ready to talk about it.

On Sunday, when we usually made the Goodwill run, Tina said she wanted to stay home. She wasn't feeling well. I was worried about her, but I was always concerned for her.

O Holy Spirit, Enlighten Me

When she got into these moods, she would quit taking her medication, and then life would go to hell again.

Later in the day, wanting to keep her in a pleasant frame of mind, I picked up a couple of lighthearted movies for her to watch and took them to her apartment. I didn't stay long. When Tina was in this frame of mind, I felt she preferred to be alone.

The next morning was Monday, March 24. I stopped over to pick up the movies that were due back. Still not feeling well, Tina didn't want to go anywhere. Tina said, "I ordered something for your birthday. It should have been here by now. I want to wait for the mail." Whatever it was, she felt it was something I needed, and she wanted me to have it. I had told her numerous times, "I don't need a thing."

For the past week, Tina's legs and ankles had been swollen. I had checked her blood pressure a few days earlier, and it was high. But considering the amount of Diet Coke she drank and the mini cigars she smoked, I wasn't sure what her blood pressure should be.

In the past few months, I had suggested numerous times that she go to the doctor. She refused. Kelly also had offered to pay for a doctor appointment for her. She refused. Like me, Tina didn't like doctors. She promised she would go when she received her disability check at the beginning of April. That was only a week or so away, so this time I didn't say anything.

She mumbled something about not needing to take the medication she was on. I was so familiar with this mood. It usually preceded her decision to quit taking the meds. I didn't stay long and left.

That afternoon, I called Kris in Louisiana. As I spoke with her, I said, "I feel as though we are going to lose Tina."

Kris was quick to tell me, "I think you are wrong. I don't feel any such thing. Once I hung up the phone, I didn't think any more about the feeling I had regarding Tina. It had completely left my mind.

I didn't call Tina on Tuesday. If she wanted to go anywhere, she would have called me. When she was in her moods of not needing her meds, it was best for me to let her alone. I only added to her frustration of having to take medication.

On Tuesday night, I picked up my phone, and for absolutely no reason, Tina's phone number appeared on my phone. I thought that was strange. I had never noticed my phone doing this before. I thought about calling Tina but chose not to. I was going to go over first thing the next morning.

The next morning, I called Tina's apartment. There was no answer. In the past, sometimes when she was off her medication, she wouldn't answer the phone. Believing perhaps that was the case, before I left for Tina's apartment, I took the time to mix her medication in the tiny container I used to slip her the medicine she needed.

When I reached her apartment, I knocked on the door. There was no answer. I tried the door. It was unlocked. For nearly fifteen years, I had gone to Tina's apartment. It had never been unlocked. I let myself into her apartment. I noticed she wasn't in the kitchen or living area. I went to her bedroom. Tina was lying on her bed. As I walked to her bed, I noticed her coloring. She was purple. My heart sank. I touched her. She was so cold and hard. I knew immediately she was gone.

I had never made an emergency phone call in my life. It took a little time for me to figure out what I needed to do.

Do I dial the area code before 9-l-l? One's mind goes blank when one walks into something like this. I was shaking as I dialed 9-l-l.

As I spoke to the operator, I couldn't remember the name of Tina's apartment complex or her apartment number. I told her the streets that intersected her apartment and said I would watch for them. Even though two days before I felt we might lose Tina, it was the very last thing on my mind that morning as I entered her apartment. I never dreamed we would lose her so soon.

I looked at Tina. It was as though she had just drifted off. Her hands were under her head. Her fingers were straight and touching, as they would have been had she been praying. She looked so peaceful. She was still wearing the same clothes she wore when I saw her on Monday morning.

Shaking, I called my husband and daughter and told them they needed to come to Tina's as soon as possible. The items I took to Tina's on Monday were still right where I set them. I believe she went into her bedroom when I left and passed away soon after, which was why the door was still unlocked.

As they removed Tina from her apartment, I could not look. I kept my back to what they were doing. I began to sob as I had never cried before in my life. There was no doubt I knew this was what God had prepared me for so many years earlier.

Chapter 12

Even though for many years I didn't completely understand what God was trying to tell me, He had taken me through this day so many times. For many years, I had known there was going to be an earth-shattering event in my lifetime. I knew this was it.

As much as I feared this day, the totally surprising thing was the way I felt in the days following finding Tina. Instead of the horrific pain I had always feared would take over my body, the only thing I could feel was Tina's complete peace and happiness. It was actually a beautiful time. I knew Tina was in a good place. I could feel her happiness and hear her laughing. As much as everyone around me didn't believe me, I also knew Tina was not going to be gone long. I knew this was a gift from God and I was experiencing something very special. This time I was not going to close my mind.

I knew this was why I always felt pregnant after experiencing the death. I knew God was sending her back to me via her sister. Tina would never be back, but I had no doubt God was sending Tina's soul back to me. Melanie was going to look after Tina, but in a completely different set of circumstances than what I had foreseen. Once again, God knew best.

I could not believe the feelings I was experiencing. I never felt closer to God. He cared enough about me to warn me so long ago about this period in my life. I felt like the luckiest person in the world. I wouldn't spend my days mourning the loss of my daughter. How could I? She hated most everything about her life. I remembered the time she told me, "You don't understand. The voices never go away." And I would wonder, "Why is the occasional voice I hear always a positive one while Tina hears voices constantly and those she perceives are destructive?" I would have to be selfish to want her back in such an unhappy life. Those voices were now silent for her. She was now happy and free.

For three days, my mind never turned off. I felt I was doing well, but I must not have been. Even though my mind was not turning off, my body must have been sleeping. The first night after finding Tina, I was awakened about three o'clock in the morning.

The voice said to me, "You can't go yet. You aren't done."

The second night, again I was awakened about three o'clock in the morning. It was the same message, "You can't go yet. You aren't done."

Did I quit breathing? I didn't feel as though I had been sleeping, but I must have been. Why was I being awakened with this message?

Because it was necessary to have an autopsy, the services for Tina would be delayed. It gave me time to deal with the shock of the moment. Kris, her husband, and their children also needed time to come home from Louisiana.

Melanie and I needed to clear Tina's apartment. It was the end of the month. Her next month's rent would be due soon. As we were busy packing her belongings, we paused for a break. I was telling Melanie how I had previously told Tina, if she ever smelled as bad as my brother (because of the smoking), I was going to tell her about it. The words were no more out of my mouth than the air freshener in Tina's apartment went *pshhhh!* Melanie and I looked at one another and laughed. I felt Tina's spirit was definitely in the room with us.

As I was gathering Tina's paperwork, one paper fell out. As I picked it up, I realized it was a balance due on another credit card. The previous year, I had taken care of her charge cards. I had written to each creditor involved, explained her situation, and believed the accounts had all been closed. I preached to her over and over again, "Don't use credit cards. I will give you the money if you need it." But as she always had in the past, she had once again opened a new credit account.

As we finished packing her belongings and headed home, we reached the intersection near my house. At that moment, I could feel Tina with me so strongly. She was so happy, and I could hear her laughing. It was such a beautiful and comforting feeling, knowing she was so at peace.

A day later, Larry's sister sent her sons and their trucks to empty Tina's apartment. It took five guys about one hour to move her belongings from her apartment to our garage. She also sent enough food for three complete meals for our entire family.

O Holy Spirit, Enlighten Me

Until I could have her mail transferred to my home address, each day I would check for Tina's mail. Kris was now home, and this time, she went with me. As I sorted Tina's mail, I would realize why God had sent Kris with me this time. I saw another credit card bill, and this one had a much larger balance due than the first one I had found. My heart dropped. I knew this was the feeling I had experienced when, less than a week earlier, I said to Tina that something was wrong. She had once again overextended herself with credit cards. Since I knew how sensitive Tina was, she wouldn't have wanted me to know. She knew I would be disappointed in her. Yes, I would have been, but I also would have forgiven her.

Another day later, I saw two credit card cases in Tina's mail, one for each of us. I knew this was the gift for me. I hated credit cards. I thought, *why would she buy something like that for my birthday?* I believe it was God's way of explaining to me what was once again troubling Tina.

Since I always felt I wanted to be cremated, we decided we were also going to have Tina cremated. I had always hated the idea of putting a body into the ground. I wanted her with me, not in the ground somewhere.

Kris and I were relaxing in the living room when I decided to clear the coffee table. The last few days had been hectic, to say the least. As I cleared the papers, I picked up the receipt for Tina's birthday ring. Until I saw the date on the receipt, it hadn't occurred to me that I bought her birthstone ring on my own birthday, the day Melanie announced she was pregnant. I believed this was God's way of again reassuring me that He was sending her back to me.

On the morning of Tina's service, I awoke with a message from God. During my sleep, He explained the signs of the cross. Catholics repeat the signs of the cross, "In the name of the Father, the Son, and the Holy Spirit." God said to me, "What we think (touch the forehead), what we eat (touch the stomach), and what we do (touch one shoulder and then the other), all must be in harmony. Before we can hear God and truly follow Him and not ourselves, all of these things must be in order. To me, this made so much sense. I understood exactly what He meant. It was exactly what He had been teaching me the last forty years.

The morning of Tina's services, I had gotten out of bed and dressed first. I was dressed in purple. When I went into the living room, I was surprised to see Kris had slept on the sofa. I had awakened her. As Kris dressed, I teased her when I saw she also had chosen a purple outfit.

The night before, after I had gone to bed, my grandson Shane arrived from Louisiana. I had not yet seen him. Realizing Shane had left Louisiana without proper dress clothing, Kris had purchased a new shirt and slacks for him. As Shane pulled his clothes out of his travel bag, I noticed he had chosen a purple plaid shirt. When I saw he too had chosen purple clothes, I told him, "Wear the clothes you brought. I want you to be you."

Then I noticed my granddaughter had chosen a tie with purple in it for her father. Dick's tie also had purple in it.

Over the years, so often Tina and I would be dressed alike. I would pick her up in the morning, only to find we looked as though we had planned our wardrobes. I would tease her, telling her not to walk with me. We looked strange, so often dressed alike. The morning of Tina's funeral, I believed my daughter had helped us pick our clothing choices.

O Holy Spirit, Enlighten Me

She probably knew I would pick up on it. Once again, I knew she was with all of us.

Since I didn't feel I could face a bunch of people, we chose to have a small service for family and a few of our closest friends. Dick's family alone would nearly fill the room for her service. I have few remaining relatives.

As we arrived at the funeral home, I shared our clothing issue with the director. As we talked, the deacon who was going to speak at the service walked into the room. The funeral director stated, "I don't believe it." When I looked at the deacon, he also had on a purple shirt and a purple tie.

As I stood in the line, greeting our family and friends, the silent voice that had become so much a part of me was now talking to me. It said, "You are going to write about this."

The day before Tina's service, Kelly had told us what he had prepared to say. The day of, when he started to speak, he had forgotten his notes. It didn't matter. Kelly could not have delivered a more perfect memorial of his experiences with Tina. I wish I had a copy of the things he said. He made her service perfect. Kelly stated he felt God had put him in Tina's life. I am 100 percent certain God put Kelly in our lives.

Tina and Kelly's relationship was more a sister-brother relationship, not a romantic one. He and Tina would often come to the house, and we played cards or went out to eat. Kelly couldn't have been a better friend than he was to Tina. So often through the years, I thanked God for Kelly's assistance in dealing with Tina. He had become Dick's favorite hunting buddy. My daughters called him their brother. I felt he was the son I never had.

Dick and I had each requested a song to be played during the service. They played the song Dick requested

I. M. Free

several times but never played "Amazing Grace," as I had requested. I wondered why but said nothing. We had arrived at the funeral home earlier than expected. I doubt they had time to get organized like they would have preferred.

When I spoke of this later with Kris, I would receive my answer. She said, "I couldn't have handled it if they played 'Amazing Grace.' They played that at Larry's funeral. It would have been too much."

After the service, everyone met at Melanie's house. I didn't worry about what we were going to do or feed our family and friends after the service. Melanie's neighbors all pitched in and helped organize things. We had plenty of food, and everything went unbelievably smooth.

We returned home after Tina's services and lunch. My two grandkids were on the sofa, teasing one another. As I watched them enjoying the moment, I would have another flash. I hadn't had one in a very long time.

Instead of my grandkids sitting there having a good time, it was my father and sister, Pat. I was very hesitant to share this with others, as I too have a hard time believing it happened, but it did. That is the beauty of God. We never know what to expect or when.

A day or so after Tina's services, I was looking at the arrangement that the family of Melanie's husband had sent. As soon as I saw it, I noticed a Willow Tree figurine in the center. They were Tina's favorites. As I removed the figurine from the plant, I noticed it was a music box. I wound the box. The tune was "Amazing Grace." That was a beautiful moment. It was as though Tina herself had picked it out at the florists, and I believe she probably did.

A week or so later, I went to lunch with my school friends. They had purchased a memorial snow globe. It too was a music box and had a space at the top for a picture of a loved one. The card I had sent to thank friends for their thoughtfulness in the previous days contained a picture of Tina. The picture fit into the music box, like it was made for it. The music box also played "Amazing Grace."

It took forty-plus years, but God explained both of my visions to me. It taught me just how loving and caring He is. I no longer fear the unknown. I know God will prepare me for anything that could upset my world. He truly took care of everything. I realize how in control of everything God is. Again it was unbelievable.

About a week after Tina's service, I went for a drive. Suddenly, the voice said to me, "I am the Father, you are the Son, and the Holy Spirit is the part of you that is reborn until you reach perfection."

I couldn't believe what just happened. That made so much sense. I got so excited and asked "Why me? Why do I receive messages no one else does?"

Chapter 13

When we received the papers from the coroner, it was determined Tina had died of walking pneumonia. That was why she had been coughing for months. Many years earlier, the psychic had told me I was going to lose someone close to me, and the person had dark brown hair. At that time, Tina was only a child and had light brown hair. Over the years, her hair had turned a very dark brown.

Today I believe God knows when He is taking us back when we are born. I know we don't have to speak out loud for Him to know what we are thinking. I believe He knows everything we are going to do long before we do it.

I have come a long way from the nonbeliever I once was. But even now, I don't like to listen to someone preach. I know I wouldn't be fooling God. He knows exactly how I feel about things, and He has been so good to me.

Before Tina's passing, I had previously mentioned to friends that I would spend the spring cleaning out my flower

O Holy Spirit, Enlighten Me

beds at home. It had been so long since I stayed home and took care of them. They were completely out of control. I had expressed concern about what Tina would do because I wouldn't be going over every morning to pick her up. God is always a step ahead of me. He already knew Tina wouldn't be here and already had something to fill my time.

It would take months for me to clear the ground cover that had overtaken my numerous flower beds. As I worked, I felt Tina with me every day during those months. It was so comforting to be able to feel her presence.

Whenever I began to miss her, I was instantaneously reminded that she would be back. God never let me dwell on the fact she was no longer with me. It was so strange. This was not at all how one should feel when he or she loses someone he or she loves. Tina was someone I had been with nearly every day for the past fifteen years. I knew I was feeling something very out of the ordinary. Again I felt so blessed.

Dick was trimming his apple trees. He wanted me to pick up the branches and put them on a burn pile. I had already made plans to visit a friend. She had lost her husband the previous year. I was not about to change my plans. I felt I was doing what I was supposed to be doing that morning. As I left, I knew Dick was upset with my decision not to stay home and help him.

When I returned, unknown to Dick at the time, he had lost his glasses and his hearing aid. As he was throwing the branches into the fire, they had fallen off his head and into the fire. When we found the glasses, they were burnt beyond recognition. The hearing aid would never be found. Although Dick is the one who goes to church every Sunday, I knew, like many, he doesn't see, nor does he hear God.

The summer passed rather quickly. It was time to plan a baby shower for Melanie and the new baby. Kris was coming home from Louisiana for the shower. When Dick and I picked her up at the airport, she wasn't feeling very well. She hadn't eaten all day. Perhaps that was why she didn't feel well. We took her to her favorite restaurant, but she couldn't eat. Her husband had been out of the country on business, and she was upset about flying home alone. I thought maybe that was upsetting her.

Dan was back the next day. She was getting worse. We told her she needed to see a doctor. She wouldn't budge. She wasn't going, and that was all there was to it.

Days passed, and she hadn't been able to eat anything or keep fluids down. Something was very wrong.

The day of the baby shower, Kris didn't go to Melanie's. She had come home for the baby shower and was too sick to attend. I went alone.

Surprisingly during the baby shower, Kris found enough strength to come to Melanie's house for the shower. She didn't look well. She didn't seem to be able to grasp what was going on around her. She seemed to be in a daze. She was determined she was not going to the doctor.

When I awoke the next morning, I had the feeling Kris's organs could begin to shut down if she didn't get help. When Dan got up, I mentioned this to him.

His reply really surprised me, "They already are shutting down. She wet the bed last night."

Dan, Dick, and I all told Kris, "You are going to the emergency room."

She was still determined she wasn't going.

Finally her father very firmly said, "Kris, you *are* going."

O Holy Spirit, Enlighten Me

She relented and went to the emergency room. She would spend the next ten days in the intensive care unit. She had infections in her liver, blood, and kidneys. She also had two types of pneumonia. She was very sick.

When we visited, we were required to wear a clean smock, gloves, and mask each and every time we entered and exited her room. When I saw her, barely any space was left in her room. It was full of machinery.

While everyone was terribly anxious over her condition, I could feel God within me so strongly. He told me Kris was going to be fine. I felt at peace inside. There was no anxiety. When Kris' daughter called to check on her mother, even though I knew Kris was seriously ill, I assured her, "Your mom is going to be fine. I wouldn't tell you that if I weren't sure."

During the days Kris was in intensive care, I could not convince Melanie she would not lose another sister. We had lost Tina the end of March. It was now September. Melanie was extremely stressed. The baby wasn't due for another month.

After nearly two weeks, Kris finally left the hospital. And as Kris left, Melanie went in. The stress was too much for Melanie. She went into early labor. The baby was born three weeks early.

When Kailee Marie was born, she made eye contact almost immediately. She smiled all the time. It seemed she understood everything we said to her. She was the happiest, most alert newborn I had ever seen.

While visiting at Melanie's a few weeks later, Kelly touched the baby on the end of her nose with his finger, something I had seen him do to Tina numerous times. At that time, Tina would close her eyes and turn her head.

When the baby closed her eyes and turned her head, just as I had seen Tina do, I knew for certain Tina was back. For me, it was a beautiful and special moment. Every time I see the baby do something Tina used to do, I realize how blessed I am. It is as though God is reassuring me, "Yes, it is her."

I feel so fortunate. I only wish everyone could experience the things I have since I found God. Then everyone would know how beautiful life on earth can actually be. It will be that way for all of us once we close our minds to the devil and follow the guidance available to us from God, if only we open our minds and let His messages in.

Death erases all of the hurtful memories or experiences we have endured. We will come back with a fresh, new outlook about life. Some of our old habits will remain, but a few of the negative traits we learned to overcome will not repeat in our next lifetime.

I no longer view death as the end, but a new beginning. Very few of us are perfect, so most of us will be reborn. Some will come sooner than others, but nevertheless, the majority of us will be back.

Our destiny lies in our hands. It is solely up to us what we choose to learn and overlook. Every cloud has a silver lining. Although my marriage didn't live up to my expectations, I don't regret things. God knew what He was doing. While many will spend their entire life leaning on their husband or wife, I know I can handle life on my own. Perhaps I would never have found God and turned to Him in times of trouble if I had been leaning on someone else.

My husband very much helped to make me the person I am. I am strong and independent. Emotionally I know I don't need another to get me through life. Whatever the future holds for me, I know God will be with me every step of the way.

I don't regret the things I haven't seen or done in this lifetime. I will have the time and opportunity to do them in the next. Nothing I could have chosen to do would have given me the peace of mind I now have. I would do everything the same way again.

Because God helped me tremendously through the thing I probably feared the most—the loss of a child—I feel I am free.

PART 2

I had written my first book two years after we unexpectedly lost our daughter. I never intended to continue writing, but God had different plans for me. It has been five years since our loss and He only recently had me continue with the writing. God said to me, "I am not asking you to convert anyone, just deliver the message." I have learned to follow His guidance and find it almost impossible not to do as I feel I am being guided. Truthfully, it brings me such inner peace. I really can't imagine not following. For me, it is the natural way to live. It is the only way I know how to live.

Chapter 14

In the months following the unexpected death of my daughter, I kept busy working outside. I didn't dwell on the unhappy times we had endured in the previous years. Instead, I focused on the good, happy times. Unlike most who lose someone they love, I didn't have that feeling of deep despair. God had prepared me for that moment in my life. I knew I was going to lose someone close to me. I didn't know who it would be. In hindsight, I should have been able to figure out it was Tina. I had said several times we were going to lose her, but my mind never really accepted it would be Tina. And, even though I didn't know for sure who it was, I knew God was going to send that person's soul back to me, which made all the difference in the world. I felt so blessed that I had been spared that horrible period of deep mourning.

Before God became a part of my life, only He knew how much death frightened me. If I had previously lost anyone I cared about, I would have wanted to be with them. I believe it truly would have destroyed me, but because God knew how deeply this bothered me, He opened my eyes and revealed things to me many people will have trouble accepting or will never believe. I will always be grateful for the messages God gave me and the peace and understanding those messages provided me. Because of His guidance, I am certain we are reborn over and over again.

When months after her death Tina was reborn to her sister, Melanie, I looked into the new baby's eyes. Her name in this life is Kailee Marie. Right from the beginning, she was so alert. I felt she knew exactly what we were saying. From the first day, she was so precious to me. I knew I was going to spend the rest of my life trying to make up for the unhappy life she had previously endured. I wanted things to be right for her. I wanted her to be happy and fulfilled. I felt she deserved a good happy life, as free from stress as possible. Of course, we can't control every aspect of another's life, but we can be there for them when life disappoints them.

I am fully aware this new baby is not Tina. She will never completely take Tina's place. The new baby is merely Tina's soul reborn. She will have many of Tina's characteristics, but she will never be Tina. This is the same soul but refreshed in a new body with a new life to live. She will have learned lessons in her previous life that will help her progress in this new life. I wouldn't want her to remember her past life. As the baby grows, I see many of Tina's characteristics. To this day, this is a beautiful thing to observe.

When my daughter Melanie's maternity leave time was over and she returned to work, I began watching Kailee a few times a week. I enjoyed my time with her. She was so pleasant. I always enjoy watching babies grow and mature. The more they respond, the more enjoyable the moment. The

O Holy Spirit, Enlighten Me

time passed quickly and I had less and less time to recall the hurtful years with my family and Tina. After a lifetime of hurt and disappointment, I was finally healing.

We were notified that our grandson, Shane, who was living in Louisiana, was getting married. Melanie's family, my husband Dick, and I purchased plane tickets to make the journey to Louisiana. Looking forward to seeing the family, we had reserved accommodations at a nearby hotel. This would be Dick's and my first vacation since losing Tina. We were looking forward to the trip. The last time we had gone, Tina had gone with us. Days before leaving, we were informed the wedding had previously been cancelled or postponed, but no one had taken the time to let us know. Thus, we made a trip to Louisiana for a wedding that wouldn't happen. At the airport, Dick would struggle to get from one gate to another. His health was beginning to slide. He was no longer able to do the things he used to do.

Even though we were disappointed no one had let us know the plans had changed, we had a good time and were glad we made the trip. When we left Louisiana for home, I told my granddaughter, Courtney, I didn't think Grandpa would be making the trip to Louisiana again.

Back home, temperature permitting, I spend a great deal of my time on the enclosed porch in the back of my house. Our backyard is very quiet, private, and peaceful. It is where I can communicate with God and seldom be interrupted. I became aware of the voice I hear beginning to put thoughts in my mind. I recalled what the voice had said to me at Tina's funeral service: "You will write about this." I knew it was time to begin putting those words into the book. I would put the thoughts that were running through my mind into my computer. This would become my first book: *I Don't Have Time, My Journey to Finding God.*

As I wrote, I wasn't sure of the order of some of the experiences, but after much checking and rechecking, as best I could, I later found most of the happenings were in the correct order.

I would write when I felt the voice guiding me. I never thought about why I was putting my life into my computer, nor what I was going to do with it when I had finished. Listening to the voice and putting those messages into my computer would dominate my spare time. It was something to do and I found it to be an uplifting experience. The voice I hear is always positive and comforting.

Many of my early experiences were very upsetting to me and had I not written the book, there were probably numerous events with which I would never have made peace. But while writing, I had to re-experience those events over and over again. It would take a long time, but eventually, many of those painful episodes would become easier to accept.

When I first wrote, I stated I was a freshman when my husband was a senior. This was an error. The voice had originally said to me I was in the eighth grade, but because my husband is four years older than me, I thought the voice was wrong. Of course, the voice wasn't wrong, I was. Just as the voice had said to me, I actually was in the eighth grade when my husband was a senior, something I was unaware of at the time of the first publishing. It was an unimportant thing, but it taught me a lesson to trust the voice over my own recollection. I would learn to trust the voice over anything else.

I had gone to the grocery store and I looked over at the lottery machine. As I looked at the lottery machine, one ticket stood out. When compared to all the other tickets, it sort of had a light or glow around it. The voice told me to purchase the ticket. Thus, after paying for my groceries, I went to the machine and purchased the $10 ticket. I usually will be patient and scratch off the numbers to see if it is a winner. For some reason, I was impatient this time. I scratched off the code, scanned the ticket, and couldn't believe what I was seeing. It said $50,000. I couldn't check the ticket a second time. If you do, the balance due will load into the machine. Excitedly, I went to my car and scratched the ticket. Sure enough, beneath one of the numbers was $50,000. I immediately tried to call my daughter at work. She was unavailable. I left a message for her to call me as soon as she could. I then went home and shared my good news with my husband. I knew immediately the money was to be used to publish my book, which I was still working on. I had the feeling I was to invest in a particular stock. When it felt like the right time, I invested in that stock. This would prove to be a very profitable investment. I updated a few things in our home and purchased a newer car. There was nothing else I really wanted. I knew the rest of the money was to be spent on the book.

I continued writing my book and months later when nearly finished, I asked my computer how to have a book published. I began receiving e-mails regarding publishing. A gentleman named David Cole began leaving me phone messages. I never answered his messages. Instead, I spoke with a lady who had sent me an e-mail. I shared with her the substance of my book. I believe she probably thought I was crazy, but we set a date and approximate time when she was to return my call.

The morning the lady was supposed to return the call, I received a phone call from an 800 number. I don't answer calls when I don't know who is calling. As I was expecting her call, I answered the phone. It was once again David Cole. He explained the reason for his call. The lady never did return my call.

Once I spoke with David, I knew immediately I was talking with the person to whom God wanted me to speak. I liked him immediately and we would have numerous long conversations. After some time, he asked if I would send him a copy of my transcript. I did so and after reading it, he said, "You have to have this published." Thus began my journey into being a published author. If not for him, there is a good chance I would have thrown the transcript into the drawer and forgotten about it. Because I credit David Cole for his encouragement and knowledge of what to do, even though I have never set eyes on the man, I dedicated the book to him. I would learn later that is not even his name as they use fictitious names at the publishing company.

When I had the book published, I struggled with the name to use as the author. I chose not to use my correct name. Because I am a private person and do not want publicity, I chose to use the pen name, I. M. Free. Once I found God, I knew I need not worry about the future. As long as I am following Him, I know things will turn out as they are supposed to. Thus, I feel free. My life hasn't been easy, but I've always been able to see others with whom I would not want to change places. As the voice guided me, I had written about my life and the feelings I experienced. I believe everything we experience is for a reason. God tests us daily. I am not perfect, but I make decisions according to how I feel. I don't try to be perfect, just honest. When I am wrong, I usually feel it and work on correcting my thinking. I get angry and sometimes will swear. I know it is wrong, but sometimes, it just helps relieve the pressure of the moment. I know God forgives me for this, and I am getting better at controlling this negative aspect of my life. If I feel someone has wronged me, I seldom raise my voice and scream at them (my husband being the exception). I think I am reasonably patient, but if I feel something is taking longer than really necessary, I will get irritated. I have never felt sorry for myself. I don't like listening to someone who feels sorry for himself. I am not vindictive or jealous. Those are two personality traits that can ruin your life. Many people let those two traits control their lives. Such a waste of time. If you want to live according to God's plan, you must grow beyond those weaknesses. More than fifty years ago, my obstetrician said to me, "Healthy mind, healthy body." Believing that made a lot of sense, it is something I have never forgotten.

I continue asking God, "Why me?" I don't ask this because my life has been hard, but because I know God has given me something very few will ever receive or understand. God prepares me for the things He knows are going to be hard for me to accept. For this, I am so very grateful. This is why I feel so blessed. I truly believe God has been good to me. Behind every disappointment or hurt is the opportunity for growth. I have grown so much since finding God, but I still have room for a lot more growth.

While others may mourn the past forever, wishing something had been different, I feel confident I did the best I could with the knowledge I had at the time. Whenever I wish I had hugged Tina more often or handled something in a different manner, I can give Kailee, (Tina reborn), a hug and kiss and be confident I am still doing my best to love her and encourage her. I loved Tina so much. We were so close, I felt all her hurt. It had been such an emotionally painful lifetime for her. She was good and very sensitive. She deserved so much more. I didn't want her to hurt any longer. I knew that life was now over for her.

When my family seemed to have a history of bad medical judgments, I decided I didn't really like doctors. I would openly state I didn't like doctors. I hadn't seen a doctor for myself in many, many years. I believe if I would have had a doctor at the time Tina was feeling ill, I would have insisted Tina see that doctor. I don't dwell on this, as I had been following God for a long period of time and I hadn't been guided to see a doctor. I believe things happened as they were supposed to happen. God had known the outcome of Tina's life for a very long time, previous to her death.

After I lost Tina, I realized, if I would happen to need a doctor, I didn't really have any idea where I would go. Thus, began my search for a family doctor. After numerous phone calls, I found a doctor that accepted Medicare patients. I made an appointment with this doctor simply because he was the most convenient to my home. Just before my appointment, for some unknown reason, I called and cancelled that appointment. It just felt like the thing to do. Shortly after my cancellation, the doctor's office was closed due to unlawful drug activity. Thus, once again, I searched for a family doctor for myself.

I didn't care which doctor I saw at the office I called, so I was assigned one. When I went for my first checkup, I immediately knew I was where God wanted me to be. I liked her and knew I was with a doctor I could trust. I soon stopped saying I didn't like doctors.

Chapter 15

When I signed to self-publish, I knew nothing about what I was getting myself into. I hadn't ever looked into anything regarding writing or publishing. I had never envisioned myself as an author or writer. I was as blind as anyone could possibly be regarding the subject.

Even though I never envisioned myself truly becoming a writer, many years earlier, I had mentioned to an acquaintance I felt I was going to write a book. It was just something I felt, not something I seriously thought about doing, especially something that would be released to the public. She was older than I and someone I respected. She asked, "What would you write about?" I answered her, "My life." She promptly responded, "Who would want to read about your life?" I had only known her for a few years and didn't have a social life with her. This person knew nothing about me or my personal life. She simply saw me as someone who didn't have a full-time job and played tennis. To this day, I find her answer amusing.

I always laugh to myself when I remember that conversation because it showed me we can see someone regularly and never really know anything about that person.

Once I signed a contract to have my book self-published, it would be the beginning of my schooling. I was in my seventies. I hadn't done anything secretarial for many, many years. I had never used the computer program "Word." I didn't know how to do anything regarding the layout, correcting spelling errors, ending a page, or beginning a new chapter. I was winging it as I went.

Once I submitted what I believed to be a finished copy, I chose to have it proofread. Thank goodness, I did that and didn't embarrass myself with all the punctuation and paragraph errors I had in my transcript. The book was on the market and available for sale within six months. Things actually went surprisingly well until it came time to advertise. Still determined not to do book signings or interviews, I was really limiting the exposure my book would get. But this sort of thing is just not me. I can't do it, don't want to do it, and won't do it. If success meant I must do these things, no one would ever see or hear about my book.

My first mistake was to tell marketing I wouldn't push the book myself. They would need to do it for me. I should never have let them know how blind I was to everything. Once the calls for advertising began, it was never-ending. It became very stressful because I was constantly being pressured to commit to one thing after another. I didn't know or have time to think about whether it was a good investment or not. I trusted the person with whom I was dealing.

My daughter warned me, "Slow down." But I felt perhaps this was what God wanted me to do. But truthfully, I could no longer hear God clearly, as I had in the past. I was stressed and always made to feel I needed to give the marketing consultant an immediate answer.

In no time, my cash on hand was gone. I committed to having an audiobook done. When I heard the audio, it was absolutely terrible. It was so obvious the person reading the words wasn't connecting with the book as it was written. I knew as I listened, she didn't get the message. Through a series of misunderstandings and miscommunication on both parts, I was told it was too late to redo the audio. Unknown to me, this horrible reading was already available for sale. I told them to put it in the trash. Thus, I lost the cost of the investment completely.

I felt I couldn't afford anything more. I had already spent more than I had imagined it would cost. But what I said didn't matter. According to my consultant, there was always something else I really needed to do. Trusting my marketing consultant, I emptied my savings account. This is making me even more stressed. This bank account was money I felt I had received from God, not my husband's and mine. I wouldn't dare ask my husband to invest in this book. He would never have done it and I would never have heard the end of it. As I know nothing about publishing or advertising, I continued to listen to this man to whom I had put my trust. Nothing was enough, I always needed to do something more. I am now cashing in most of the stock I have remaining. Oh, but again, there is one more thing I really should do. I felt pressured, but after signing too many contracts, I foolishly would sign one more contract. Now I am in over my head. A day or two at the latest, I tried to get in touch with my marketing consultant. I wanted to cancel the latest contract. Of course, he was in a meeting or something and didn't take or return my call. When he wanted something, he had no problem calling me as late as 9:45 PM or on a Saturday. When I finally spoke with him, which was about five days later, I was told it was too late. Things had progressed too far, I couldn't cancel. Thus, unknown to my husband, at seventy-seven years of age, I now have a home equity loan.

Once I finished the communication I needed to complete my latest investment, in my mind, I was done speaking with this man. But very soon, I received yet another call regarding something he felt I really should do. For me, this was the last straw. I feel I can no longer trust him. He has absolutely no idea how much stress he is putting in my life. I don't doubt his intentions were in the right place but I now believed he was willing to see me penniless, divorced, or on the street, to sell me one more thing. I felt taken. I truly believe this person meant well. I just wish he had listened when I said I couldn't afford something and respected my words. I blame myself for letting someone control my better judgment. Lesson learned. I had put my trust in someone whom I really shouldn't have. I let him take over my life. I was no longer in control. Beware! I have not included this in order to be vindictive. I have included this for the benefit of anyone who is considering self-publishing or any other endeavor which involves someone else advising you how to run your life or invest your own money.

I felt I had only invested my own security. It was money from God. My husband has worried about money during our entire marriage. He would never have spent money on publishing and advertising this book. He knows I have spent all of my money, but I wouldn't dare ask him to also invest.

I think of the marketing consultant every month when I make my home equity payment, praying my husband doesn't find out. To console myself, I tell myself perhaps God really wanted me to invest in the things I invested in. I really don't know at this point. Time will give me that answer. I want to believe I made that last investment because it was God's will. Regardless of the outcome, I still believe I will receive my rewards in my next life. That reward is not necessarily monetary but will be a happy, content life, free of worry and stress.

Feeling the need to set myself free, I put the book into my past. I didn't want to concentrate on something that might never happen. It really didn't matter one way or another. I was exhausted and I knew I needed a break from worrying about the book. Certainly, I would like for someone to purchase the rights to it, but it isn't something I think about or worry about. I know God has a plan and I need only wait for Him to share that plan with me. It is completely in His hands. I really do feel free.

Chapter 16

It is springtime and Kailee is now about 2 and 1/2 yrs. old. She is very observant. There isn't much that gets past her. She picks up on things I can't believe a child her age notices. We are outside and live rather close to a fire station, so sirens are often heard when outside. I have heard her father tell her the police are going after the bad guys when they have their sirens on. In the past, when Kailee heard a siren she told me, "They are going after the bad guys." Today, when she heard the siren, she told me, "I am a bad girl because I poop my pants."

Dick is having prostate problems. Unknown to me, he urinated outside in my flower bed. Kailee pointed and announced, "Grandpa peed there." I couldn't believe he had done this in front of her. She knows what Grandpa did was wrong and now believes when she hears the siren, they may be coming for Grandpa.

Months later, Dick would be diagnosed with prostate cancer. After finishing the series of radiation treatments, he would be hospitalized with urinary problems. He was sent home with a catheter. When Dick talked with his doctor, he was instructed to remove the catheter. Not realizing how the catheter had been inserted, Dick yanked it out of himself. He bled profusely. Kailee was with me that morning. I called for assistance, the sirens came up our driveway, and this time they did take Grandpa.

Only three years old, Kailee shares many of her mother's traits. Melanie has always been athletic and it seems Kailee is also going to be a natural athlete. Melanie and Lance would take Kailee bowling. She went up and pushed the ball down the lane. Drawing the attention of others around their lane, she is pointing and screaming as the ball rolls down the alley, "That way, that way, go that way!"

She had taken swimming classes over the winter. It is once again summer and I would take her to my friend's to go swimming. She continues to become more and more comfortable in the water. She loves the water and looks forward to going. Dick doesn't like the water and doesn't swim. He would accompany us and talk with his cousin as we were enjoying the water. He is having trouble with his leg, which since his open heart surgery many years ago, has always been swollen. He seldom feels like doing anything around the house. Everyone is telling him to exercise, but he has no incentive to listen. He spends the majority of his time playing cards on his computer and watching television.

I awoke one morning and Dick is having trouble getting his breath. He called his doctor and his doctor suggested he go to the hospital. He would be admitted with congestive heart failure. He had recently been diagnosed with type two diabetes. It is just one body function failure after another.

I. M. Free

I had hoped the years of spending my time going to doctor appointments, emergency rooms, and hospitals were behind me, but again, I was wrong. I begin to feel Dick isn't going to be with me forever. His health has steadily been getting worse every year. He has always been a complainer, so I can pretty much ignore his constant and never-ending complaining. I wish he wouldn't do it, but for the most part, I can block it out. I feel God is preparing me for the future when I will be on my own.

My granddaughter remains the light of my life. In the fall, Kailee celebrated her birthday. A video was made of her blowing out the candles while everyone sang "Happy Birthday." Today, she is playing with her other grandmother's phone and watching the video. Again, today, someone is taking videos of her. As she watched the video on Grandma's phone and everyone is yelling, "Blow out the candles!" Kailee started blowing into the phone, trying to blow out the candles. It was hilarious. This precious little child makes me so happy.

At forty years of age, Melanie has decided she isn't having any more children. She would have a garage sale and put her baby clothes and items into the sale. She sold a few items, but many items were not purchased. Although Melanie believed she was finished having children, Lance wasn't so sure. He wanted another child. They had a hard time conceiving the first time, thus it seems improbable they would have another child without medical assistance. But God had other plans. Before summer's end, Melanie would become pregnant a second time. Among the items that had not been sold at the garage sale were most of the necessary items for having a second child.

Shortly after Melanie announced her pregnancy, I began feeling my husband's passing. I have always felt I would outlive him, but now I am beginning to become aware of how my life would be when I am alone. In reality, I feel I have almost always been the one to carry the responsibility of organizing and caring for our home so I don't really feel overwhelmed. He has never paid the bills, done the laundry, washed the dishes, cleaned the house, cared for the flower beds, and has only very, very occasionally cooked dinner. In fact, the only thing he does is mow the lawn and clear the driveway in the winter. Should I pass before him, he definitely would be overwhelmed.

It is the fall of the year and I went to lunch with a friend. On this particular day, I could feel Dick's passing very strongly. It was as though it had already happened. Because of the feelings I had in my early thirties, I am not particularly shocked at experiencing something like this. I have already learned it doesn't mean it is going to happen soon. I never really know for sure when something is going to happen. It happens when it is supposed to happen, but God prepares me in advance. This is something for which I am very grateful. Again, it is what makes me feel free.

For months, I believed Dick was going to be reborn to Melanie, but during the Christmas holiday, God told me I was wrong. I didn't really know whose soul was going to be reborn to Melanie.

Weeks later, one evening as I lay in bed talking to God, I would receive the most beautiful message He could deliver to me. I was shocked. I couldn't believe what I was being told. I knew it came from God because it was something that had never ever crossed my mind. I was told the soul would be that of my mother. I lay in bed with a great big smile on my face. Once again, I feel like the luckiest person in the world and I am totally aware of how hard this is for others to believe or accept. I am always aware of how unbelievable the things I say are to others, but I also know sharing my messages is what God wants me to do.

While discussing reincarnation with my mother many years ago, she had told me if we are reborn, she didn't want to come back for a long time. It was approximately thirty years ago that my mother passed away. While my mother was still here, I had purchased a necklace for her. The necklace was a dove and on the reverse side was the message, "O Holy Spirit, Enlighten Me." I had also purchased the same necklace for myself. After her passing, I would wear my mother's necklace and was very disappointed when I lost the dove. It had come off the chain. After I lost my mother's necklace, I would start wearing the one I had purchased for myself. Nearly ten years after my mother's passing, I would plunge the toilet. I couldn't believe it when my mother's dove reappeared. It was now tarnished, but I was still so glad to see it again. It also made me believe God was telling me we do come back.

As Melanie neared the end of her pregnancy, the doctor was going to do a sonogram. Melanie wanted Kailee to see the baby, so Kailee and I met Melanie at the doctor's office. Melanie was going to visit with the doctor after the sonogram, so once Kailee saw the pictures, she and I left.

On the way home, Kailee and I stopped for ice cream. Soon after we arrived home, Melanie called the house. Her blood pressure was too high. She needed to go to the emergency room.

O Holy Spirit, Enlighten Me

I had invited Tina's longtime friend, Kelly, for dinner that night. Kelly had been part of our family for years prior to Tina's passing and has remained one of us. Having just had ice cream, I wasn't really hungry, but I set the table for Dick, Kelly, and myself. As I wasn't really hungry, I assumed Kailee wouldn't be hungry. She usually ate dinner later with her parents, thus I didn't set a place for her at the table.

As Kelly, Dick, and I sat down to eat, Kailee came to the table. Knowing her father would be picking her up soon, unthinking, I said to her, "You aren't going to eat right now." Without a word, Kailee left the table and went into the room.

Lance arrived and we were deep in conversation about the happenings of the day. As we spoke about the circumstances and viewed the pictures of the sonogram, Melanie was still at the hospital.

As Lance prepared to leave, I asked, "Where is Kailee's backpack?" Unknown to me, she had picked it up and gone out the door. She was ready to go home. Concerned about her mother, I knew I had been ignoring her. She came back into the house and as she made eye contact with me, I could see I had hurt her.

That night, when I could not sleep, I thought about the evening's events. I realized I hadn't even asked Kailee if she was hungry. I had previously had a conversation with myself about not ignoring Kailee once the baby arrived. It was something I felt I had done previously to Tina. Compared to her older sister, Kris, Tina was such a good baby. Because Kris required so much of my attention, I felt I often ignored Tina. Over the years, I felt perhaps some of the trouble I had with Kris was due to my own mistakes as a mother. I didn't want to repeat those mistakes. I was upset with myself. The baby wasn't even here yet, and I was already ignoring Kailee.

The next night, after Kailee had returned from preschool, I went to Melanie's and apologized to Kailee.

I told her I was sorry I hadn't asked her if she was hungry and asked, "Why didn't you tell me you were hungry?" She replied, "I did." Knowing I had really screwed up, I told her, "I'm sorry. Next time, tell me again until I hear you. I am a bad grandma." Her reply was adorable. She smiled at me and said in the sweetest little voice, "No, yer not."

One week later, Melanie was sent to the hospital because again her blood pressure was too high. This time, it was determined they would induce her labor. As with Kailee, Melanie was once again going to deliver early. Kailee had been with Dick and me for the day, thus she accompanied us to the hospital. On the way to the hospital, Kailee, with all the innocence of a child, stated, "Mommy is going to poop her baby out." I laughed so hard. How can I not love this child? The next day, Melanie gave birth to a beautiful little girl.

Chapter 17

When the new baby, Jenna, was born, Melanie had decided it would be too much for me to watch both children. Before she returned to work, she had made plans for Jenna to go to daycare each day, while I would watch Kailee on Mondays and Fridays. That sounded like a good idea to me. At seventy-seven, I don't feel I can watch two small children full time. It was decided when Kailee entered kindergarten, I would then watch Jenna a couple of days a week.

Melanie had plans so she dropped off the children. We put Jenna in the pack-n-play and she lay quietly. As Melanie left, I walked with her to the car. I had only been outside a few minutes. When I re-entered the house, Dick met me at the door carrying the baby. This is a man who has unexpectedly fallen twice in the past two weeks and he doesn't have enough sense not to pick up the baby. "Why are you carrying the baby?" He answered, "She was crying." I could only shake my head.

I remembered when he was pushing snow out of the driveway. He asked me to stand on the snowblade for added weight. I could only lean against the hood of the tractor. There was nothing to hold on to. He backed the tractor up, reversed gear, and drove the tractor as fast as he could into the pile of snow he had previously pushed aside. He hit that pile of snow and I went flying. I could not believe he was that thoughtless.

Shortly after Tina had passed away, he asked me to help him move a trailer filled with mulch. As I assisted him, he let go of the trailer, leaving me with the entire weight of the trailer and mulch. I never felt anything so strange in my life. I honestly felt like my insides were going to come out of me. For my assistance, I received a double hernia, which years later, I would have to have repaired.

Last summer, when he asked me to hold onto a tri-pod that held a huge flowerpot so he could adjust it, I had the sense to say, "No, I learned my lesson. I don't listen to you anymore."

After many, many months of not being able to do much of anything, Dick would have back surgery. We recently had three trees removed and new grass planted. I was raking the excess straw off the new grass as Dick sat and watched me work. He told me to put the straw in the garden space, as we didn't have a garden this year. "Don't put the grass in a pile, spread it around over the garden area." I shot him a look. He responded, "What is the look for?" I replied, "There is nothing I do that you don't tell me how to do it or I do it wrong." Dick replied, "I am not telling you that you do it wrong, I am just telling you how to do it." I replied, "What is the difference? After fifty-six years of being told how to do things, it is getting harder and harder to listen."

O Holy Spirit, Enlighten Me

I am not without my own faults. I like to change things around my house. My husband hates change. In the early years of my marriage, my furniture seldom was in the same position for more than a week. I remember my own grandmother constantly straitening things in her home. I guess in that respect, I am just like her. I often change things and Dick doesn't even notice, but when he does notice, he is angry. But I seldom change something that Kailee doesn't notice. When I move the furniture, she'll ask, "Did you do it yourself?" and the answer is always, "Yes, I did it myself." Today, I rotated the throw rugs in my kitchen. When Kailee walked in, she commented, "I like your triangle rugs." She is only four-years-old and she notices which rugs I have in the kitchen, and how does she know it is a triangle design?

Kailee and I were sitting on the swing in the backyard. We had spent the summer searching for toads, which she would play with for a short while and release. She is never happy with only one. We always have to look until we find at least two. It reminded me of Tina who would always have to have two birds, cats, or fish. In Tina's mind, there couldn't only be one. They had to have company. As we relaxed, I mentioned to Kailee that I accidentally hit a toad last week when I mowed. She paused and her non-typical response from a four-year-old was, "That's a bummer!" Her answer made me laugh. No one says, "That's a bummer" anymore. I asked her, "Where did you hear that?" Her serious answer, "I know a lot of things you don't know I know."

We knew for a couple of weeks that our nearly fifteen-year-old parakeet was not going to be with us much longer. It was very apparent he was failing. Fifteen years is very good for a parakeet. One afternoon, I walked into the kitchen only

I. M. Free

to find my parakeet floating in the dishwater. He probably was flying to reach the window and didn't make it to the ledge. When my four-year-old granddaughter found out the parakeet had died, she said to me, "If you had taken better care of him, he probably wouldn't have died." I chuckled at her observation. I was just reprimanded by a four-year-old. I always enjoy the responses I receive from Kailee. It lets me know that she is very alert and aware. I am certain she will do well one day.

Dick asked Kailee what she did yesterday. He knew she had spent the day with her other grandmother and grandfather. Kailee was trying to watch a cartoon on TV. Dick often tries to interrupt her as she watches the TV. He does it to annoy her. Without taking her eyes off the television, Kailee responded, "Nothing you need to worry about."

Dick asked me, "What did she say?" I spoke up and said, "I think she said, nothing you need to worry about." With her eyes still glued to the TV, Kailee stated, "That is what I said." Kailee is no fool. She knows when Grandpa is trying to annoy her and she isn't afraid to stick up for herself.

It has been weeks since Dick's back surgery and he is finally able to begin physical therapy. This morning, Dick had an appointment with the physical therapist. When he returned home, he was complaining about how much he hurt. He immediately called the doctor. It is approximately 9:30 in the morning. When he hadn't heard from the doctor or his office by 1:00, he called a second time. When Dick is in pain, he thinks of nothing else. In his mind, he is the only person in the world that is hurting and the doctor should have called him by now. It reminded me of the time he met the dermatologist in the parking lot without an appointment and before her day had even begun. I was so embarrassed he did that that it would take me years to make an appointment for myself with the same dermatologist.

It has always been stressful living with my husband, but now that he is seldom feeling well, it is getting even more stressful. He has never been able to carry on a meaningful conversation with me. Trying to have a conversation with him, I told him about a big limb that had fallen off the tree in the backyard. When Dick saw the limb, he said, "That's not a big limb." The limb was about twenty feet long. It seems Dick always has to disagree with me. His answer irritated me and I thought, but didn't say out loud, "I didn't say the tree fell down."

A few days later, as we left to go to his doctor's appointment, he snapped at me, "You're going to get in the grass." I have been driving out of our driveway for more than forty-five years. I think I know where the driveway is and anyway, I don't care if I do get in the grass, but I let his comment pass. As we reached the end of our street and I turned right, Dick said, "I would have gone the other way." It didn't really matter which way we went, we would arrive at our destination about the same time. Is he trying to drive me crazy?

After a couple of months, it was decided Dick needed second back surgery. Needing clearance from each of his doctors, Dick had four doctor's appointments that week. The pre-admission testing alone took nearly three hours. I have spent too much of my lifetime at hospitals and doctor's offices. It drains me just to go there. That night, as I talked to God, I knew in my heart I couldn't do this much longer. It was the same feeling I had prior to Tina's passing. I felt I just couldn't do this much longer. I wondered, "Is he going to be here much longer?"

I felt I needed a break before another surgery. I wanted to get away. I hadn't been anywhere in years. I needed some space to think about other things and breathe. Melanie knew I had wanted to go to Put-in-Bay for several years so she volunteered to take a vacation day and take me to Lake Erie before the surgery. Melanie, Kailee, and I headed to Lake Erie. Jenna, the baby, would spend the day as she usually would at day care.

My nephew's fiancée owns a very nice Bed and Breakfast on the island. I hadn't seen it and was looking forward to surprising my nephew. Melanie would drive my car. On the way to the lake, my engine began making a noise. We had no idea what could be wrong. The engine and oil lights didn't come on, so we kept driving. We made it to the lake, got on a ferry, and headed to the island. The car was the last thing on my mind. I needed to relax.

After a very relaxing day on the island, we again boarded the ferry to return to the mainland. We weren't ten minutes into our trip home when the engine died. We would be towed to the nearest dealership.

When we arrived at the dealership, Melanie made the statement that this was all Kailee's fault. She was the one who wanted to take Grandma's car. I immediately said to Melanie, "Don't do that. Don't make Kailee feel guilty. It wasn't her fault. The car didn't have that many miles on it. It was the car's fault. It never should have broken down." The dealership was closed, but a gentleman said he was there to close a deal and he offered to take us to a nearby vacation resort where Melanie's husband would make the two-hour drive to pick us

O Holy Spirit, Enlighten Me

up. We left the car there, as it was going to be very expensive to have it towed home.

On the day of surgery, Dick and I left the house at 10:30 AM. His surgery was to be at 1:00 PM, but because of an operating room delay, the surgery didn't take place until 3:30 PM. Around 6:30, we were notified he was in the recovery room. It was nearly 8:30 PM before we were allowed to see him. Melanie and I went in for a short visit. Just coming out of sedation, Dick was his usual argumentative self. When Melanie announced she and Kris were going to buy him a lift chair, he nastily stated they weren't to do that. It had been a very long day. I was exhausted and all I wanted to do was get away from his tone and the hospital. I was ready to go home and left shortly thereafter. The hospital staff could accompany him to his room when they were ready. The surgery went well and he was stable. That was all I needed to know. The next day, I was too exhausted to go to the hospital. I knew what I would hear when I went in and really didn't need another day of his mood.

The next morning, Dick called me at 9:30 AM and told me to come get him. As he was talking to me, a voice in the background said something to him and he said he would call back. About 11:30 AM, he again called and said to come pick him up.

I went to the entrance where he told me to pick him up. I sat there for over an hour. Finally, I went in a second time and inquired as to what was taking so long. I was told they had taken Dick to the main patient pickup, which was not where Dick told me to pick him up. I had asked him two times at which entrance I was to pick him up. Yet, when they had taken him to the main entrance, he said nothing to them.

When he finally got into the car, there was a long period of cursing and complaints from him. According to him, it was the worst morning ever. He was waiting to leave and his nurse kept going up and down the aisle. She wasn't doing anything. Through Dick's eyes, he was her only patient. I am so aware he certainly does live in his own little bubble. I would later learn the delay in releasing him was because the nurse didn't feel he should leave the hospital yet.

My car would be at the dealership where we left it for nearly a month. Unknown to me, the man we spoke to at the dealership wasn't a salesman but the owner. My car had less than sixty thousand miles on it. I had purchased it secondhand and didn't have a warranty. Once we were notified the manufacturer had no intention of assisting with the repairs, the dealership owner stepped in, made a phone call to the right person, and the manufacturer offered to replace the engine if I would pay for the labor, which cut the cost in half. I was more than happy to do that. I thanked the dealership owner and God for taking His foot off my back. I felt much lighter.

My lack of concern regarding the engine knock would cost me thousands of dollars, but I am so tired of life that I just don't care about the engine or the expense. When life craps on you hard enough and long enough, you can always turn it over to God. That is what I did. I don't have the energy to get angry or upset. It is just a car and only money. There are so many more important things in life. Someday, some way, it will get paid. I hate owing money, but sometimes, life is beyond our control.

Chapter 18

One month after the car broke down, Kailee said to me, "It is my fault your car broke. I am the one who wanted to take your car." I immediately replied, "No, no, no, Kailee, it was not your fault. The car should never have broken. It was the car's fault." Why is she even thinking about the car? She continues to amaze me with what comes out of her mouth. I am so aware she is always thinking about things.

Even after Dick's second surgery, he was in a lot of pain. He seldom speaks. He just sits, leaning over, trying to relieve the pain he feels in his back. There is nothing I can do for him. I am not sure this surgery is going to change Dick's life all that much. The surgeon said he could stabilize his spine. But with all arthritis and degeneration that has taken place, I have my doubts this surgery is going to help. I know Dick wants to have the ability to do the things he used to do, but that is not reality. I believe the days of hunting and tinkering in his garage all day are probably behind him. He just hasn't accepted that.

Needing a change of scenery, I have to leave the house daily. I want to get out and speak with others. I can forget how much I dislike my life when I am around others. Dick barked at me, "You think you have to go somewhere every day." I answered him, "Yeah, why would I want to leave when I could stay here all day, listen to you complain, and watch you sleep?" I left and before returning, picked up some lunch for Dick. He was sitting in his new lift chair when I handed him his lunch. He asked, "Would you get me a drink?" Disgusted, I asked, "Don't you get up at all anymore?" His answer was, "No, not if I don't have to." I answered, "You aren't an invalid, but you sure are making yourself one."

I am so tired, but no matter how tired I am, I am always aware there are so many people who have lives tougher than mine. Nevertheless, I think it's perfectly normal to wish our lives were happier and less stressful. God's road is a long road and the last days before change always seem the hardest. The other night I went to sleep feeling I just couldn't keep living my life without some sort of positive change. I feel that change is not far away and I suspect there is probably going to be some pain along with that change. I felt as I did just before Tina passed away. At that time, I felt I would rather leave this life than keep doing what I was doing. As much as I loved Tina, I felt I just couldn't do it any longer. This is the way I feel about my life with Dick, except I am not ready to leave this life.

Kailee is spending the night tonight. She keeps me from dwelling on what may be to come. She is always uplifting for me. She is a constant reminder that death is not the end, only a

O Holy Spirit, Enlighten Me

new beginning. My life is all about making Kailee and Jenna's lives better than the lives they experienced in their previous lives. I feel so blessed that God has opened that window for me and I know, even though many doubts me, this is what life is all about.

My life has been hard, but I have never felt sorry for myself. Self-pity is not an attractive personality trait. Self-pity is the person that constantly dwells on their own misfortune and is jealous of those who enjoy a more comfortable or prosperous lifestyle. I am constantly aware of those with whom I do not wish to change places. I am always aware my life could be so much worse. We all have days when we verbally wish things were different. I don't view this as self-pity. I have to admit I am looking forward to better days and hope to see those days in this lifetime.

It has been three weeks since Dick's second surgery on his back. He is as negative as always. He says he is still in pain and he's not any better. I can see for myself that is not true. He is better, but he is such a negative person he thinks he isn't any better. It is hard to listen to him complain day after day. He has been complaining for approximately twenty-five years. It has gotten old. I feel no sympathy for him. I believe he brought so much of it on himself because of his outlook on life. Between worrying about his health and money, he can never appreciate all the good, positive things going on around him. For me, he is depressing to be around.

When I married fifty-six years ago and I said my vows, I promised till death do us part. I have recently rethought those words and what they mean to me. I meant the vows when I said them and have worked at keeping my marriage together. But there are times when I feel if I stay married, it is going to kill me. I am not willing to die just because I feel I must stay married. Today, those vows mean if staying is going to kill me, I really should move on and get away from the thing that is killing me. There are days when I feel as though someone is sitting on my chest and I am not able to breathe normally. That is how much stress is in my marriage.

The love in my marriage died many years ago. These days, I think we just tolerate one another. I will never marry again believing it will be forever. It will be until the reasons to leave are greater than the reasons to stay. There comes a point when people should just admit they shouldn't still be trying to make something work for the sake of making it work. There has to be love, respect, and truly caring about the welfare of the other person. When that is all gone, why stay?

There are several reasons why I stay. Number one being that is not where God is guiding me, and I don't want to hurt anyone. Because of the money I have invested in publishing a book, I can't afford to leave or even take a small vacation. I feel trapped and I did it to myself. I let someone talk me out of nearly all my savings. It isn't as though Dick and I don't have money, but I know Dick feels the money in our savings is his money. He would have a fit if I took money out of our savings to take a vacation, especially since he knows I have spent what I considered to be my money. Life is about learning and growing. I have learned a lesson and hope to never let anyone put me in this situation again.

I spend some of my time thinking about my life, what I did wrong, what I did right. I want to leave this life with a clear conscience, knowing I did the best I could. I hope I have many good years ahead of me and I am looking forward to those years. I feel I have done my best with my marriage, even though it has been far from perfect.

This Thanksgiving, I began thinking about something that happened to me nearly thirty-five years ago. It is the one thing in my life with which I had not made peace. I was sexually assaulted by someone. It is something I have kept buried in my mind, not wanting to face it. But I know it is time and I am determined to face it and make peace with it. After much thought, I realized it was time to forgive that person and set myself free. Only a few of my very closest friends know of this and no one knows what happened, only that something happened. I am glad I never spoke about it openly. It would have embarrassed and ruined lives. Not everyone will handle things the way I did and I would never suggest someone handle a similar situation the way I did. This is one of those things that each person must listen to his or her conscience and deal with it in their own way. But by Christmas of this year, I truly forgave this person and I am freer because of choosing to let go of something that could in no possible way ever be changed. It happened and it was time to let it go.

Chapter 19

This past year, Dick and I became great-grandparents for the third and fourth time. We have two grandchildren and four great-grandchildren in Louisiana. I am certain Dick doesn't know what sex the new babies are, let alone their names. His entire thought process is about himself and the way he feels. He doesn't seem to realize other people are experiencing their own problems and challenges. Sometimes, he is talking with someone who I am aware has serious problems also, but Dick seems oblivious to their life or struggles. He too often thinks only about his own discomfort.

He has always been oblivious to my challenges in life. Early in our marriage, he had told me he didn't want to hear anything about my family's problems. When most of my family was dealing with their illnesses or problems, Dick never asked how they were doing or gave any thought to what I was going through as I tried to help them. It was very disappointing, but I knew this was just the way Dick was.

O Holy Spirit, Enlighten Me

After so many years, you learn to accept people with their faults. You cannot change them. You only can change the way you feel about them.

When I think back, I probably came across the same way when I began having visions I didn't understand. All I thought about for quite some time was what was happening to me. I know I talked about it a lot. So, I guess as the saying goes, what goes around, comes around. I needed time to find myself and I need to understand. Dick needs time to find himself.

In my first writing, I wrote I would do everything the same way. I say that because I have been following God for many years and I have lived my life according to the way I felt God was guiding me. My life hasn't been perfect, by a long shot, but it was the life God chose for me. I often wonder what type of person I was in my last life to deserve the life I received this time. I am sure I have received the life I deserved, whether it be good or bad. I can only do my best this time, in hopes I will receive my rewards in my next life. I have always had the attitude if my bills are paid, I am happy. Certainly, I'd like more, but that is all I really need in order to find inner peace.

There is seldom a day I spend with Kailee that she doesn't say something that makes me chuckle. I enjoy her company. She seems to always say or do something that makes me happy inside. This morning, as I went into my office to use my printer, I looked down, and there, hidden between my file cabinet and the desk, was the candy dish. She had hidden it from Grandpa. Kailee knows Grandpa isn't supposed to eat a lot of candy. Even though she had hidden the candy dish, she won't eat the candy without first asking if she can have a piece.

I. M. Free

I keep a picture of Tina, her dog, and me stuck in the glass of my secretary desk in the living room. Today, Kailee had removed the picture and was carrying it around. She asked me who was in the picture. I told her it was my daughter Tina who had died, her dog, and me. Kailee then asked me where the dog was. I told her the dog died also. She asked, "Did Tina come back?" I told her, "Yes." She asked, "Did you die?" I answered, "Yes." She asked again, "Did you come back?" Again, I answered, "I am here." Still curious, Kailee asked, "Where is the dog?" I answered, "I don't know."

The entire conversation shocked me. I had promised myself long ago not to interfere with Kailee's beliefs. I want her to find God, as I did. I want her beliefs to come from God, not me. I haven't said anything to her about reincarnation. So, where were all these questions coming from?

Dick's back has finally healed to the point he is no longer complaining constantly about how badly it hurts. He is very weak from being pretty much immobile for nearly two years. But instead of working out and building up his strength, he would decide he isn't going to therapy any longer. He said, "I just do the same things over and over again. They tell me what to do, and I have to do all the work." Everyone is telling him how well he is doing, but he still feels he isn't doing well.

I said to Kelly, "I wonder what he will complain about next." It didn't take long. Dick would begin urinating blood. He would once again see his doctors. He has since stopped bleeding, but at the beginning of the year, he is to have a procedure to help diagnose the cause.

Yesterday, when Dick got up, the first thing he told me was his hand fell asleep last night and it hurt so bad, he had to get up. The first thing out of his mouth this morning was,

"My legs itch so bad I can't stand it. Can you find the cream to put on them? I looked and I can't find it." Before bed that night, he asked me to look at his back. He said it felt as though the cut from his surgery was wide open. I looked and all I could see was the scar from the surgery. When it comes to his body, it seems he can always find something to worry about.

The following day, he told Kailee to go get his shoes and socks. I was in the bathroom doing my hair and hollered out, "Go get them yourself. You need the exercise." Kailee didn't go after his shoes and socks. I have always hated the fact Dick thinks others should wait on him. I remember when Dick and I were only dating, he would tell his younger sister and brother to go get things for him. It is something he doesn't do for anyone else.

Thank God I have Kailee to brighten my day. She doesn't know it, but she is saving me from insanity. She was looking for her paint set. I told her I must have thrown it away. She said, "I must have used it all when I was a kid." I said, "When you were a kid? What are you now?" Her response, "I'm a bigger kid."

It is the Christmas season and Melanie called and was telling me while she was shopping, she saw a woman she felt was in distress. Melanie asked the woman if she could help her. They spoke and the lady, who Melanie believed was near ninety, told her she had lost her job after forty-seven years and the only place she could stay with her dogs was at the Roadhouse. She said she had to keep moving, as she couldn't afford her arthritis medicine. Melanie asked how much she needed. The lady stated she had fifteen dollars, but needed another twenty. Melanie opened her wallet and gave the lady the money. Melanie asked, "Did I get taken?" I told her my

I. M. Free

gut feeling was she did the right thing. I told Melanie, "Don't worry about it. God will give you the money back." A few hours later, Melanie bought a lottery ticket. She had wanted to purchase the Christmas ticket from the machine, but it wouldn't work, so she bought the ticket next to it. She won $500. A few days later, Melanie was telling a friend about her experience. The friend showed her a picture on her cell phone, asking Melanie, "Is this the lady?" It was.

For weeks, Dick has done nothing but sit in his chair and either sleep or sit motionlessly. He either doesn't eat or he eats very little. His back is no longer inhibiting him. There is no reason he can't be doing things around the house or go to his garage. I have done my best to deal with his moods all of my married life, but the past two years are taking their toll on me.

In the past when he has gotten deeply depressed, I have called his sisters for assistance. I can't keep doing that. The last time I tried to reach them, neither sister was available. People have their own problems. I can't ask others to save him. He has to want to do it himself, and apparently, he doesn't want to. I am not angry, nor do I feel sorry for him. I know how he has used the fact that he was the wage earner to control me. Years earlier, I said to him, "Whenever I worked, you didn't. You always made sure I didn't have any money." The look on his face told me I was right. It seemed whenever I worked, Dick would find a reason not to work. Nearly all of my checks went to pay household bills because his checks would always be short of the amount needed.

When I went to sleep last night, I had my usual talk with God. I was so tired of my repetitious life, I began wondering about the choice I made when I won the $50,000 lottery

O Holy Spirit, Enlighten Me

ticket. I had spent the money on publishing my book. At the time I had the money, I felt I could either change my life by leaving my husband or I could invest in the book. As I felt I was to publish the book, that is what I did.

I was rethinking that decision. I had a hard time falling asleep and I never entered a deep sleep. Very early the next morning, I felt something wet under my finger. I turned on the light to see what was wet. There was a spot of blood under my finger on my bedsheet. The spot was about chest high and was about the size of a quarter. I got up and looked over my body, trying to find where the blood came from, but I wasn't bleeding anywhere. I got a washcloth, cleaned the spot, rinsed the cloth, and again scrubbed the bedsheet. I kept wondering from where the blood came. A short time later, I took a bath, checking my body in the mirror, and again, I wasn't bleeding anywhere.

I went about my usual morning routine. When I took a break and sat down to relax, it again crossed my mind, why was there blood in my bed? Almost immediately, the voice that I hear stated, "He died for you." Once again, I could not believe what was happening to me. This just doesn't happen. I had to share this with someone. I called my friend, telling her of all the hard-to-believe things I have told her, this is going to be the hardest to believe. I made arrangements to meet her at her house and went to share this experience.

I was almost crying. I just could not believe what had happened to me. I told her, "I can't tell people this. No one will believe me. This just doesn't happen to ordinary people." She didn't reply to my words. Instead, she said, "I believe you."

I had previously arranged to have our routine card game with friends that evening. I revealed to one other friend what had happened. I couldn't say anything to anyone else. I felt so strongly, no one will believe me. I have a hard time believing the things I experience. If I heard someone say the things I say, would I believe them? To be completely honest, the answer would be probably not.

After much thought, I realized God had just assured me I made the right choice when I chose to publish my book.

Chapter 20

At Thanksgiving, I predicted Jenna would be walking by Christmas. She was walking before Christmas. Jenna is only ten months old and she has no teeth, but she is walking. She is so alert it is hard to imagine her just sitting in one place or crawling. It seems so natural for her to be walking. She is adorable. I can see she is going to have a mind of her own. She will be making life interesting for a long time to come.

It has been nearly two weeks since Dick ate a sufficient amount. He is so light-headed and weak, he can hardly hold himself up. Still, he went to his usual Friday breakfast with friends. At this time, I really don't think he should be driving, but it would do me absolutely no good to suggest that he not drive. When he came home, he said he couldn't eat breakfast.

Dick's cousin called to tell us her husband had fallen on the ice. He was in intensive care with five broken ribs. He has had multiple health issues and the last thing they needed to deal with was broken ribs. He is in extreme pain and they were keeping him comatose. As they are two of our closest friends, Dick and I are very concerned about both of them.

Dick and I would spend Christmas day at Melanie and Lance's. While Dick has been sleeping almost non-stop, he stayed awake long enough to call Paula twice to check on her husband. He joined us at the dinner table and after eating a small amount, he once again retired to the sofa. He sat down and asked me to get him some water. I said to him, "You can't even get your own water?" His answer once again, "No, not if I don't have to." While Lance and Dick slept a good portion of the day away, Melanie and I cleaned her bedroom so she could put her Christmas present, a new rug, down. We spent a very quiet Christmas day.

At home the next day, Dick and I listened to a CD of piano music. It is beautiful, relaxing music. We listened to it over and over again. Paula is still dealing with her husband at the hospital. I am totally at peace. For some reason, I feel as though a load has been lifted off me. I am not angry at Dick; there is nothing more I want to say to him. I am tired of the endless fighting to live my life as I want to live it, versus the way he wants me to live my life. At this time, I feel I could lose my husband and our friend.

God prepares me very well. I feel things over and over, until one day, it finally does happen. I know when it happens, I will be ready to let it happen. I said to Melanie the other day, "Why do I have to go through these things over and over again?" Melanie answered, "Until your daughters are ready to let go." And, I know she is right. Because God loves all of us, He will prepare all of us as best as He can before He takes Dick into his next life, if that is His plan.

O Holy Spirit, Enlighten Me

Dick hasn't eaten a significant amount of food for a very long time. He is extremely weak. I made him an egg and toast, yogurt, and a nutrient drink. I told him if he wants to live, he will eat whether it tastes good to him or not. I can't do anymore. He would eat some of the yogurts. I am so exhausted from dealing with his never-ending illnesses. I have turned him over to God. At this point, it is entirely between Dick and God. I can live with the outcome regardless of what that outcome may be.

I wonder, was what I feel the death of my marriage or Dick's actual death? At this point, I really don't know. I just know if I am going to survive, I have to have a change of lifestyle. I don't want to continue living the way we are living and I am not ready to leave this life.

It is December 31st. Dick called his doctor's office and told them his symptoms. I accompanied him to his doctor's appointment. The doctor seemed surprised Dick was going to have a procedure in a few days. Dick had led me to believe the doctor had suggested it. After thoroughly examining Dick, the doctor suggested he go to the emergency room, as his offices were closing at 1:00 PM. He wouldn't have time to get the results from blood tests in that short of time. On the way to the emergency room, I called Dick's cousin to check on her husband's condition and to let her know we would also be at the hospital. Her husband is still comatose and it is not looking good. I am concerned about Dick, but I am not happy about spending another day of my life in a doctor's office and an emergency room.

At the emergency room, Dick would be thoroughly examined once again and they also took x-rays. He was diagnosed with a little bit of pneumonia in his lungs. It was nothing for which he need be hospitalized.

As we left the hospital, he is suddenly hungry. He had this miraculous recovery in a matter of minutes. His voice is no longer weak and deathly. He wants mashed potatoes and coleslaw, but he doesn't think he would be able to get the chicken down. We picked up the food he wanted on the way home. I watched him eat. He ate the food, including the chicken, so fast I am surprised he didn't eat his fingers. I am suddenly disgusted and angry. I realized he wasn't as sick as he wanted me to believe. I felt so manipulated. Between the doctor and the emergency room visit, it was clear, Dick was not nearly as sick as he was appearing to be. He has had me worried for more than two weeks, making him three items for breakfast the previous day, telling him he has to eat or he is going to die.

After finishing his dinner, he was once again back in his chair. He decided he needed a glass of ice water and asked me to get it for him. I got the water, restrained myself from throwing it on him, and gave it to him with a look that said, "Don't ask me to do another thing for you."

When I went to bed that night, I was angry at God. What was the past couple of weeks about? What was the purpose of this? I truly believed Dick was seriously ill, but now I can see that was not so. He basically has a cold, but he acted like it was so much more. I had begun taking notes about what Dick was doing after Thanksgiving. I felt it was another of those things I was to do. I had done that and God had let me believe Dick was truly dying. Why did God do this to me? I knew God and I were going to have a serious talk that night. It was New Year's Eve.

O Holy Spirit, Enlighten Me

The following morning, I knew. During the night, God made me see my life in an entirely new light. I am aware of how I have let my husband dictate my life for most of my married life. Certainly, I fought his control, but still, I let him do it. My lights are finally turning on. I have told my friend for years, when I married Dick, I married the devil. We have been going in opposite directions from the very beginning. Whenever I wanted anything, I had to literally fight for it. Nothing from Dick was given to me out of love and respect. If I didn't fight for what I wanted, I received nothing or it was done Dick's way. I have felt all my life that marriage should be forever. Well, overnight, God has set me even freer than I was previously. I faced the fact I don't love my husband and haven't for many, many years. I was brain-washed since childhood that marriage should be forever. Last night, God made me see that only I have been working to make this marriage work. Dick very, very seldom does anything to please me. He doesn't even know how to, because he is the only person he is concerned about. My purpose is to serve him. All I want is out, and because of my previous investments, that is presently impossible. If I hadn't written things down the past month, I would never have seen what was happening. God had truly done this to me for my own good.

I said nothing to Dick. Discussing things with Dick never changes a thing. He isn't about to change. He is the way he is and I have accepted that for years, but now I have definitely had enough and I want more for myself. I know God is going to open that door for me. I only need to wait for it to happen. I have no idea how or when He will do it, but it doesn't matter. I know He is going to do it.

In the days following my enlightenment, I realized many things about my life. When I married my husband, I had him on a pedestal. He was good-looking and a very good athlete. People liked him. He could be very charming. Women found him attractive and would flirt with him. But after I married Dick, I found he wasn't really interested in my life. He was jealous of most of my friends and would get upset with me when I did things with them. He pretty much controlled me until I started playing tennis. By that time in my life, I no longer cared if he didn't like the fact that I was enjoying myself with my friends. As Dick aged, the women no longer fussed over him. He began to change and became harder to live with. It seems everything was downhill after that.

I often stated he acts like someone who never got enough attention as a child. And when I look at his home life, I am certain I am right. There were four boys and three girls and his mother was raising them by herself. Dick's father had died when Dick was in high school and Dick was the second oldest. His mother worked every day. Of course, she didn't have time to give them individual attention.

After days of thinking about my life, I know I no longer want to be married to Dick. He hasn't thought about anything but himself most of his life and especially for the past two years. I feel he truly is a hypochondriac and he is making himself sick. He has nothing to talk about except how he feels, and if you ask, that is never good. I believe this is an illness and something Dick is not even aware he is doing to himself. But I also know I cannot help him. I just know I want to be free. At least, I now have a plan. I just must wait for God to make it possible. Again, I asked myself, "Has God been preparing me for Dick's death or the death of our marriage?"

At this time, I really don't know, but I feel I am not supposed to dwell on that. God has a plan and I need only live my life one day at a time and continue following God's will each day.

The next day, we went to the hospital to check on our friend. He is still at comatose and has never awakened. It still doesn't look good. I am still very concerned about both of our friends.

I would spend the next day taking my Christmas decorations down and storing them. It has been a rough couple of weeks. I feel we are reliving the Biblical days. Our friend is carrying his cross. He cannot wake up and communicate. That has to be hell for him because I am certain his soul is very aware of everything that is going on around him.

It has been weeks since our friend fell and was hospitalized. He is still not wakening. They have to make a decision about what to do next. He has had multiple complications. If he survives, he probably won't be the same. My advice to Paula was, "Don't think about what you want, think about what your husband would want." I concluded, "I believe if he passes, he won't be gone long. One of your granddaughters will become pregnant and he will be back soon. I wouldn't say this if I didn't believe it with all my heart and soul." I am concerned about Paula, but I know she is extremely strong. It is going to be very, very hard on her, but I know she will come through this. Unfortunately, a little more than a week later, her husband would pass away.

Chapter 21

The day before our friend's funeral, Dick would have a procedure done regarding his urinary problems. I asked him to delay the procedure, as I thought it would cause him to start bleeding again and I wasn't going to miss the funeral. Impatient as usual, Dick went ahead with having the procedure done.

The morning of our friend's funeral, I drove to the funeral. Dick and his sister were with me. Dick Is helping me drive as usual and told me where to turn. I didn't listen, as he was wrong. I was somewhat familiar with the church we were looking for, so I kept going. As it seemed most of the cars were going to the church we were looking for, I was following the traffic. As we entered the parking lot, Dick is pointing and telling me where to park. Irritated with him, I barked at him, "I don't know why God gave me a brain because I have you to do all of my thinking for me." Dick proceeded to tell his sister about a disagreement he and his brother had the previous evening. Dick was angry at his brother. "You can't

O Holy Spirit, Enlighten Me

tell him anything. He always thinks he is right." Dick's voice raises as he is explaining this to his sister. I had listened to Dick rant about this very thing the night before. Not in the mood for this particular conversation, I asked Dick, "Why do you always have to be right?" In this instance, Dick was the one who was right. I went on, "Even though you know you are the one who is right, can't you let him believe he is right?"

After the funeral, we would spend the rest of the day with friends and family. When we went home that night, I was exhausted and went to bed. I had just begun to relax when Dick stated he needed to go to the emergency room. He was having a problem. I know the problem is not serious and I am tired. "I am not going anywhere, take yourself to the emergency room." He did and was home a few hours later.

A few weeks later, a mass is dedicated to our friend. I would once again drive to church. As I left home, I was told which way to go. I know where the church is, but I need to go the way he would go. I listened to him and went his way. As we entered the parking lot, I was told where to park. When we left the church, it was a snowy, rainy night. The weather is somewhat distracting. Dick turned the radio to an uncomfortable volume and directs me on how to leave the parking lot. At home, I usually back into my half of the garage. He told me I was going to hit his truck. I was watching in my rearview mirror. When I got out of the car, I was approximately one foot away from his truck. I normally would have moved over and given him even more space, but by now, I am totally annoyed with him. I got out of the car and stated as I entered the house, "You are a pain in the ass!"

A couple of weeks after her husband's passing, Paula wanted to go to the casino. This is her way to relax. She enjoys it and usually does pretty well. Knowing she needs a break from her routine, Dick and I accompanied her to the casino. I have previously stated if I go to the casino wanting to win, I will usually lose. I have found that when I go for someone else, not greed on my part, I will usually come home with most of the money I left with.

I wanted to go, but I also wanted to go for Paula. I came home with $700 more than I left home with. Thus, when a couple of weeks later Paula wanted to go again, I was happy to go with her. Before we left, Dick told me he didn't have any money and asked if I would give him some money. He knows I won the last time. I handed him a $100 bill.

A day or so later, I had gone to the store and when I came home, Melanie was in Dick's garage. She hollered for me to come out to the garage. While I had been gone, Dick had told her where he kept his money in the garage. Something I suspected he had hidden out there but was never sure. As she counted his money, he had nearly $2,000. A week earlier, he had told me he had no money. It was so obvious Dick would much rather lose my money than his own when we go to the casino.

The last couple of years have robbed me of my patience with Dick. Since the first of the year, I am so much more aware of how he tries to control every aspect of my life. I just want to be free to be myself and not feel every moment I need to do what pleases him. I went to bed and asked God, "How much longer do I have to live with this? I just want it to stop."

I was just thinking and didn't really expect an answer. I was surprised when the voice promptly said, "It is going to be a while." Disappointed with the answer, I decided I wasn't going to talk to God for a while. I hadn't closed my mind to

O Holy Spirit, Enlighten Me

God since I lost my sister many years ago, but I am tired of my life and I want it to change. I am getting impatient. If I had any money with which to live on, I could make that change. God knows that, and leaving is not part of His plan for me, which is why I feel I probably don't have any money of my own.

The next day, I went to lunch with friends and shared with them my previous night's conversation with God. They know me pretty well and are probably never really sure what I may say. I don't think they are too surprised by my conversations with God. I've been making comments for years.

Even though I wanted to close my mind to God, that night, I would receive an explanation. I was told I must learn to accept Dick the way he is and not let it upset me. I thought to myself, "It is going to be a long while because that is not going to be an easy thing for me to do."

As much as I'd like to just close my mind and do my own thing, I can no longer do that. In my heart and soul, I know God is guiding me in the manner that is best for me. Even when I have tried not to listen and do my own thing, it didn't work. It only made things worse. Hard as it is, I just have to remain patient.

I continue my conversations with God. Since the first of the year, God has made me see things I had never been able to see or understand. He explained to me I was the only one trying to make this marriage work. He has since explained Dick has always been jealous of my friends. Dick has always believed because he was the one bringing home the money, I owed him. It wasn't our money, it was his. It wasn't enough that I paid the bills, cooked the meals, washed the clothes, cleaned the house, cared for the kids, took them to their activities, mowed the lawn, washed our vehicles, and helped him build three houses. I wasn't bringing in any money, and to him, that was what was important.

I made two decisions on my own in the past year. I decided I wanted to get away before Dick's surgery. It wasn't something I felt I should do. It was something I wanted to do. I made that decision. When my car broke down, that decision cost me thousands of dollars. I also had sixteen hundred shares of a stock that had only moved pennies in the time I had owned it. I had my daughter cash out half of it and put the small amount of money into my savings account where it remains. I then had my daughter cash out the remaining stock. That cash is still in the investment account. I never had her transfer it to my savings account. I was still concerned about the money I owed on my home equity loan. God never told me to spend it on that loan. Thus, it is still in my savings account. Since then, that stock which I no longer own has more than quadrupled in value. Another lesson learned. I will wait for God to tell me what to do with this money. I pay for my decisions in a negative way.

I had a conversation with one of my school friends. She has dealt with numerous disappointments in her lifetime. I have said to her several times she could write a book about her life. Her response was, "There are too many things I don't want to think about."

That is exactly why we perhaps should write about our lives, even if we never share it with anyone. For me, it has been what God has guided me to do. It was not something I actually chose to do. I was very hesitant to disclose to the world what my life has been about. As I continued the conversation with my friend, I told her, "I believe what we don't make peace with in this life time will come back again in our next life until we learn what it is that God wants us to learn." My mind is so much freer because of writing about my life. It made me face things I otherwise would never have dealt with in this lifetime. I will never be sorry I faced the early years of my life and made peace with all the painful moments.

Chapter 22

Jenna recently turned one year old. I predicted she was going to have a mind of her own and so far, that seems to be the case. A couple of times, I have kept both girls all day while mom and dad are working. The first time I had them all day, Melanie called about 10:00 AM to see how things were going. Both girls were sound asleep. Melanie asked me not to let Kailee sleep for more than an hour. I heard her but preferred to ignore her request. I am not getting any younger and I still have my mind about me. If the girls want to sleep, you better believe I am going to let them sleep. Kailee slept four hours and when she awakened, I asked her to wake her sister. Not wanting to hear Melanie's reprimand over the sleep time, I never mentioned to her how long Kailee slept. I believed the unexpected sleep time was a gift from God.

A few weeks later, I once again have both girls. Jenna is running a slight temperature and won't be going to nursery school. She was very good until she became cranky and didn't want to take a nap. She did the phony cry that babies do when

O Holy Spirit, Enlighten Me

they want their way. I was holding her and just laughed at her. She stopped whining and looked at me with a look that said, "What are you laughing at?" When I just smiled at her and told her I knew what she was doing, she began the whiny cry again. Again, I just laughed at her. Again, she stopped and looked at me with a puzzled look on her face. She soon laid her head on my shoulder and fell asleep. Babies understand a lot more of what we say than people want to believe.

The next evening, Melanie and Lance wanted a night out and asked me to again watch both girls. This time, I am still a little worn from the previous day and not really up to chasing a one-year-old all over the house. Jenna is into everything. She was into my kitchen cabinet, opening drawers, tearing up magazines, fighting with her older sister, pulling the protective pads from the hearth of the fireplace, grabbing the briquettes around the fireplace logs, spilling her sister's milk into my living room carpet, and dropping cereal everywhere from her cup. A couple of times, I thought she was going to go headfirst into my bathtub. She was like an out-of-control tornado. I was exhausted. She is adorable and I love her tremendously, but I am not up to this. Kailee is so easy to watch; she has spoiled me. Jenna is another story. I can only hope these are temporary times and in time, she will outgrow her determination to do things her way. Kailee was not this way.

After watching the girls the other evening, I noticed the figurine that I'd had sitting on the coffee table was missing. Upon searching, I found it behind the couch. Kailee had taken it and put it there for safekeeping. It was such a small thing, but it made me once again see how thoughtful and special she is.

I. M. Free

I seldom think about my first book. I always believed it would not go anywhere while Dick is part of my life. I periodically receive an e-mail regarding advertising, but I usually ignore them. One gentleman called numerous times and left messages regarding advertising and promoting my book. I didn't return his calls. I am hesitant to trust anyone at this time. I am already in debt from my last attempt at promoting the book. I have learned a lesson and it doesn't feel like the right time. I believe when it is time, I will feel it in my body, as I did when I wrote the book, won the lottery, invested in a particular stock, spoke with David Cole who convinced me to publish the book, and also when I found my present doctor. These were events I was certain were God's will. At the time, I could feel in my body I was doing the right thing.

God has spoken to me continuously since I wrote the first book. I know He had me do it for a reason. He continues to guide me to become a better person and I believe I am continuing to grow. I don't know why, but I feel it is just not time for me to financially promote the book. I feel confident God has a plan. I know I must remain patient. So, once again, I just put the book out of my mind.

It has been a long but mild winter. I am not an outdoor person when it gets cold. I prefer the warmth of the sun. Spring weather is finally approaching and it will be nice when the weather warms and we can be outside again. With the change in weather, I have the urge to clean things. I realize the day when I will be unable to physically do some things is going to catch up with me and I want to get my life in order. I have gone through most of my things and gotten rid of those I know I will no longer use. I would love to do the same with Dick's things, but I know that would only cause another

O Holy Spirit, Enlighten Me

argument, so I let his things alone. Dick has a garage through which there are only a path and a room full of hunting gear in the basement. I have no idea what many of his possessions do, let alone what they are worth. When it comes to touching his things, that is totally out of bounds.

Dick has pretty much done nothing but sit and sleep for over two years. Although I no longer believe it is just a physical condition hampering Dick, it is what he seems to want to believe. I have tried to point out to him numerous times I don't want to leave all of this for our girls to clean out when we are gone. Kris lives in Louisiana and Melanie has a full-time job and two kids. She will not have time to clean out the garage. To me, it only makes sense that we begin to think about the future and get our lives under control.

Dick has a desk in our family room that is his. He gets irate when I touch anything on it. It is always a mess and is something that every time someone walks in the front door, is in full view. He was out of the house one day and when he came in and I had removed everything from the top of the desk, he was so angry I feared he could have hit me. His reaction made me even angrier than he was. I shouted, "I am only dusting it! I was going to put it all back." I have not dusted that desk since. When it gets too dirty, I set the dust cloth and spray on it and tell him it is time to clean it.

During my entire marriage, every time I cleaned a space, Dick would bring something home and fill that space. At the present time, we have four desks in the house. Yet, last fall, Dick had Kelly put another desk in our garage.

I found someone who could use a desk and gave it away. It had been in the garage all winter. When Dick found out I gave it away, he screamed at me, "That was not your desk to give away. You always have to have your way. We do everything the way you want!" I shouted back, "I told you I didn't want that desk in my garage before you put it there. You have an entire garage full of things I am not allowed to touch. If you wanted it, you should have put it in your garage. Oh, yeah, there isn't room in your garage." The person who wanted the desk changed her mind and it is still in my garage.

While cleaning out my own drawers, I came across a message from a fortune cookie. The message was, "Patience makes lighter what the soul may not heal." I felt it was a message from God and tried to understand why I had found it when I did. What was God trying to tell me? It would take time before I would understand. But after much thought, I realized God was telling me I really need to stop getting upset with Dick and my life with him. If I make peace with my situation now, it will be easier for me to accept later. I understood what God was telling me, and I am trying to adjust my thinking.

I know it will not be easy, but I am determined to once again understand what it is that God wants me to learn. As I know getting along with Dick is going to take some time, I try to stay out of his space. I have spent a lifetime of. If I say it is hot, he will say it is cold. If I say it is sunny, he will say it is cloudy. It's hard to believe I have spent my life with this. I am tired of the constant bickering and want to go my own way and live in peace, but for now, I have no choice but to deal with it.

I hadn't received this message any too soon. My life and that of almost every human being were about to change. We were about to experience a pandemic on a level that is almost unimaginable. We were about to hear a lot about coronavirus.

As a resident of Ohio, we would become among the first states to be asked to remain in our homes. All unnecessary businesses would be closed. Only grocery stores, drug stores, and gas stations are to remain open for business. We are being made aware of cleanliness as never before. We are asked to remain 6 ft. distant from others, wear masks when among others, and wash our hands frequently.

When a friend called and told me she sprayed her bed with Lysol every night before going to bed, I began to laugh. "What are you spraying for? Bedbugs? Fleas?" She paused and said, "Are you telling me I am being foolish?" Laughing hard, I replied, "You haven't been anywhere; no one has been near your bed. Where is the virus going to come from?"

While most see this pandemic as a health and economic event, I see it as God speaking to us. We have become a very spoiled society. We take so many of our privileges for granted. Many live beyond their means and have put nothing aside for tomorrow, while others don't make enough to make ends meet. We too often forget those who are in dire need. If this doesn't become a wake-up call, I wonder if anything will ever make people question their priorities. I can't help think about all of those who don't have enough food or know where next month's rent money is going to come from.

While everyone is making adjustments to the way we live, we received a notice from Dick's union regarding receiving his monthly retirement check. They sent a notice written on bright pink paper, asking retirees to please sign up for direct deposit so they would be sure to receive their check. When I mentioned to Dick what they requested, he immediately was not going to do that. "I like it the way it is. I don't want to change it." His instant negativity disgusted me. Because he believes it is me requesting the change, it sent him immediately into a reverse state of mind. He wasn't going to do it. Disgusted with him, I replied, "I wouldn't marry you again if you had all the money in the world." I was done talking to him. I turned him over to God.

I left the check on the kitchen table. Let him do what he wants to do. I am done with it. Surprisingly, after I didn't look at him or even stay in the same room with him for a couple of days, he asked me, "If I fill out what I can fill out, will you finish this and send it in?" Of course, I took care of it.

After that verbal outburst, it seemed Dick's mood changed somewhat. About a week later, I noticed he became less disagreeable. I can only hope it lasts, as we don't know how long we will have to tolerate one another without being able to escape our home. Only one month ago, Dick was upset because I leave the house daily. Now, I have no choice but to accept my life as it is and stay at home.

Because of God's warning, I am determined to learn to live peacefully with my husband. I will never be able to go back to where we were when I married him, but I must learn to stop letting him push my buttons. I believe I have grown since I married Dick, but I also feel he is pretty much the same person he was when I married him. When not angry with him, I am able to see this is just who he is and I feel sorry for him.

With the change in lifestyle, Melanie and her husband will be working from home. As their childcare is now closed, they will be trying to work while tending to two children. That would not be easy to do. Thus, I will be spending more of my time babysitting.

When Melanie dropped the girls off, she was telling me how to cut Jenna's food into portions she could swallow. I smiled at her and said, "I know, I raised three girls." I spent the week watching Kailee and Jenna at my house. They were unbelievably pleasant and it wasn't nearly as exhausting as I thought it might be, but definitely is not something I would want to do on a regular basis.

Still too chilly to be outside, we hung a swing on the back porch. We had installed it temporarily when Kailee was small. It is once again hanging and the girls have kept themselves entertained playing with the swing. When Kailee wanted me to go outside with her and play hide-n-seek, I told her, "Kailee, Grandma is too old to play hide-n-seek."

During the past year, Kailee has reminded me numerous times that I am seventy-seven. Having had a birthday, Kailee knows I am now seventy-eight, but according to Kailee, I went from seventy-seven to eighty-seven. I told her, "Kailee, don't be telling people your Grandma is eighty-seven. I am seventy-eight."

Chapter 23

Kailee helped me clean the birdbath in the backyard. In front of the birdbath is a plaque in memory of Tina. Kailee asked me what it said. I told her, it was in memory of Tina and says, "It broke our hearts to lose you, but you didn't go alone. Part of us went with you the day God took you home." Kailee asked, "Did she sleep long?" I answered, "No." Kailee asked me, "Did she come back?" I answered, "Yes." When my aunt had died, Kailee was with me as I attended calling hours. I had told her that she was sleeping and went to see God.

A while later, as Kailee asked Dick a question, she preceded the question with "Dad," but immediately changed the question to "Grandpa." In the past, she has called me "Mom." Sometimes I wonder, does she subconsciously remember some of her past? I really don't know but it makes me curious. I believe as she gets older, I will get that answer.

What surprises me is that she questions life after death, even though it is not something I have ever discussed with her.

O Holy Spirit, Enlighten Me

I wondered where these thoughts are coming from. Did she overhear her mother talking about my beliefs? I am certain it is nothing that Melanie has spoken about with her. I am very aware that Kailee listens to discussions that don't involve her and she absorbs what she hears.

There is nothing like a coronavirus quarantine to make you look at your life in a completely different light. When I looked at the big picture, it made me realize how small my complaints with Dick actually were. Although I haven't changed my mind about a change in lifestyle, I realize how very fortunate I am compared to so many others. I have a home in which to live, we have enough food, our bills are paid, and thus far, our family members are all healthy.

Unbelievable as it is, Dick changed a great deal in a very short time. He has stopped being so argumentative, is sleeping a little less, and actually mowed the entire lawn, not just the front lawn, as he had been doing.

I asked myself: Has Dick actually seen the light somewhat about where we are in our lives, or is it because I am home twenty-four hours a day, seven days a week, which is what he has always wanted? Or is this God's work? I don't have that answer right now.

When I turned Dick over to God, I truly stopped suggesting to Dick what I felt we needed to get done around our house. It had never worked. Every time I suggested something to him, he went into reverse. Once I turned him over to God, it was as though God put a zipper on Dick's mouth. He became much more pleasant. Dick suggested I put three of his lawn care items on the internet for sale. This was something I had asked him to do more than a year ago. After he sold those items, he was ready to sell the enormous pile of lumber he had taking up space in the garage. When the lumber was sold, several of those people were interested in his tools. He told them he would call them when he was ready to sell them and knew what he wanted for them.

Dick needed to move a few things in the garage so the lumber could be reached. He hadn't done anything physical for years, thus when finished, he was hurting. After the man purchasing the lumber left, Dick sat down on a bench near his garage. Kailee wanted to sweep the garage where the lumber had been sitting. As Kailee and I swept, I turned to see Dick lying flat on the driveway. I didn't know if he passed out, fell, or just laid down. When he didn't move and made no attempt to get up, I became concerned. I didn't have the strength to help him so I moved the bench closer to him to help him get up. Without any explanation as to what happened, he went into the house.

Kailee and I continued sweeping the garage floor. When finished, I loaded the dolly Dick had just emptied with some of the lumber still sitting on Dick's table saw. I was just throwing the lumber into a pile on the dolly. Kailee didn't like the way I stacked the lumber and pushed the pile onto the floor. It was a pretty good size pile. I found her reaction amusing. She restacked the lumber into a very neat and stable pile. Sometimes, I just can't believe how mature she is for five years of age.

I have my bath products placed in certain places for my convenience when I take a bath. Kailee had rearranged things. This morning, I thought to myself this is something Tina would have done. Kris and Melanie would never think to do something like that. A couple of years ago, Kailee moved the wastebasket in my laundry room. I had kept it in the same spot for as long as I had lived here. I actually liked it better where she put it and have left it there ever since.

When Melanie dropped Kailee off this morning, I could see immediately Kailee wasn't her usual self. She looked and acted tired. She wasn't active like she usually would be. She was more sensitive than usual and she said to me, "I want to stay with you forever." I smiled at her and said, "Don't worry, I am not going anywhere. I am going to be here until you get old."

While Kailee and I watched television in another room, Dick came into the room and started his usual tormenting of Kailee. She just wanted to quietly watch her cartoons. Dick, as usual, is totally oblivious to anyone's feelings except his own. When he didn't stop, I said to Dick, "She's not feeling well. Let her alone." As old as Dick is, he can never sense someone else's mood. It is one of those things about him I dislike a lot.

When a friend called, I went into another room to talk with her. Kailee soon came over, sat on my lap, and fell asleep. Kailee weighs fifty pounds. I didn't have the strength to move her and knowing she needed the sleep, I sat and held her for about an hour.

When Kailee awakened, Dick was in the other room working on a small puzzle. Kailee went over, ran her hand through the puzzle, and knocked it into pieces. I didn't yell at her but told her that wasn't a nice thing to do. She was acting spoiled, but in my heart, I felt I could understand why she did what she did. I believe Kailee's reaction was out of frustration because Dick is unable to see or feel when she isn't up to dealing with his own need to have attention. I can say that from experience.

Kailee has always been hesitant to have physical contact with Dick. She very seldom wants him to hug her. She will play games with him and talk to him, but she draws the line at physical contact. It is my belief her soul remembers how he treated her in her past life. Dick never paid any attention to Tina. He never understood schizophrenia. Dick believed Tina could control her mood and always seemed to hold it against her that she was the way she was.

Have you ever met someone and disliked that person immediately? I believe this is because perhaps this person was in your life previously, or the person reminds you of someone you didn't like. I have always felt this is why Kailee dislikes physical contact with her grandpa. Even though Kailee doesn't remember the past, I believe her soul remembers how he treated her previously.

Melanie found a daycare that has been allowed to remain open during the quarantine. Thus, we are back to our schedule of Jenna being at daycare daily, while I watch Kailee on Monday and Friday. Again, the weather is wet and cold and we aren't able to be outside. Dick tormented Kailee, as usual. It annoys me that he can't speak to her without teasing or tormenting her and asks her the same ridiculous type of questions over and over again. As she tried to watch television, he repeatedly threw a blanket onto her. Without looking at him, she would throw it off. Again, he asks her the same question over and over. It is so obvious he wants attention. Finally, I said to him, "You can't talk to her without picking on her. Just have a normal conversation with her." I feel like I have two kids in the house fighting. By evening, I couldn't stop myself and complained to one of my friends about my day. I felt I was doing so well handling my patience with Dick, but I slipped.

For about one month, I didn't complain about my husband. Yesterday started off on the wrong foot. I was up and dressed and he asked, "Are you up?" This is a typical observation from Dick. I have always found it annoying when he asks me a question and the answer is obvious. It goes along with, "Are you home? Are you doing your hair? Are you making supper?" These are regular questions from Dick when he can already see the answer. For years, my response has been, "No, I'm milking a cow." I ask myself, "Why is this getting on my nerves when he has always done this? Should I have pointed out years ago this is very ignorant? Would it have made him stop anyway? The answer is probably not. He is the way he is and has changed very little in fifty-seven years of marriage. I think the answer is because for the past couple of years, he has done nothing but complain and watch me do most everything.

Dick and I seldom watch the same television shows, thus he is in one room, and I am in another. Dick is hard of hearing and usually has his television at an uncomfortable volume. I get so tired of asking him to turn it down so I can hear my own. Today, I turned my volume up higher than his and left it up. He soon came around the corner and looked at me. I turned my television down and asked him, "Did you get the message?" He didn't say anything, but went and turned his volume down.

Last week, I had taken Kailee swimming at Paula's. On Friday, Kailee asked me, "Will Larry be back?" Her question really surprised me. I guess because we had recently been at Paula's, she was thinking of Larry. He had passed approximately six months earlier. I told her I believed he would be back. She asked, "How?" I answered, "I believe we come back as babies." I paused. "You are going to get me into trouble." She asked, "Why?" My answer was, "Because not everyone believes what I believe." I am sure I only caused more questions in her little mind, but I don't want her father and his family to believe I am putting thoughts into her mind. She asks me and I answer her with what I believe. It does put me in a strange and uncomfortable position. I have to wonder, why is she so curious about this particular subject? This is not the first time she has brought this up. It definitely is not something I bring up when I am with her.

Chapter 24

I was going to go pick up a new storm door that needed to be replaced on the porch. Dick decided he was going to go along, so he drove his truck and I went with him. I got into the truck and turned the heater off. It is 73 degrees outside, but Dick has on a fleece jacket. Dick immediately said, "Don't turn that off, I'm cold."

We made it to the lumber company without any problems. Dick is having trouble with his bowels and had been to the doctor earlier in the day. On the way home from the lumber company, he needed to use a restroom and pulled into a gas station to use the restroom. He then wanted to go to the drugstore to pick up his latest prescription. I was half out of the truck when it started backward. I pulled my leg back in and waited for him to park. I didn't think too much about what had just happened. When I came out and got back into the truck, he just sat there, staring at the gear shift. I asked him, "What is wrong?" His answer was, "Nothing." Still, he sat there staring. Again, "What is wrong?" When he left the parking lot, he missed the exit and drove four feet into the grass and over the curb. "What is wrong with you?" "Nothing." We drove past a park and he was in the grass. I clapped my hands, as though he was in a trance, and screamed, "What is wrong with you?" "Nothing." On the next street, he rode the guard rail for about twenty-five feet. Again, I screamed, "What is wrong with you?" His answer was, "I am ten feet away." "No, you aren't!" As we entered our own street, there is a car parked in the street. It was as though he didn't even see the car. I screamed again, "You are going to hit that car!" When we got home, I screamed, "There is something wrong with you. You shouldn't be driving. I am never riding with you again." Again, his answer was, "I was ten feet away!" He is so bullheaded. I know something is wrong, but he is never going to tell me what it is.

Before 8:00 AM the next morning, Dick was ready to hang the storm door. I remembered five years ago when we replaced another door. He had a horrible time figuring out how to hang it. Before we even began, I knew this was not going to go well. I stated, "We should wait till Melanie is around. She is younger and stronger than we are." Melanie is out of state and won't be back for a week, but of course, we have to do it now. Dick has almost no strength. He began taking the old door down. We got the door down, and now have to figure out how to hang the new door. The doorway is plumb, but a little too wide. We need a filler about 1/2" in width. He cut a board and it was five inches short of the needed length. I pointed out he needed to cut one smaller piece to fill the gap. His answer was, "I am going to center it." I pointed out he would have a gap at the top and another at the bottom. We did it his way. I told him, "My back is killing

O Holy Spirit, Enlighten Me

me. That door is heavy for me to hold while you are trying to fit it." When hanging the door was finished, we have a gap at the top and bottom and also a half-inch gap at the opposite top corner. He proceeded to put a filler strip at the top of the opposite side and two smaller strips to fill the gaps in the original strip. We built three homes, but it took two and a half days to hang a storm door. By now, I am so frustrated with the way the door has been installed, I don't want him to make another repair around the house.

Still thinking about the trip a few days earlier, Dick stated, "I am not going to quit driving." I answered him, "You could kill someone, but it won't be me, because I am never riding with you again."

A week later, after Melanie had returned from Tennessee, he told her sometimes he can't focus. He couldn't tell me that but he would tell Melanie. Why wouldn't someone who couldn't see ask someone else to drive? Why take a chance? He can't focus and still thinks he should be driving. God, he is bull-headed. He has since had regular doctor's appointments and thus far has asked me to take him to them. I pray he has enough sense not to drive, but I can never be sure.

What am I to do? I know he is having some sort of problem, but lots of times, older people begin to lose touch and there is nothing you can do to make them understand they are no longer functioning as they should. Dick has always been extremely bullheaded and it doesn't do any good whatsoever to point out he isn't capable of doing some things any longer. I can only hope when I am unable to do as I used to do, I can recognize that fact.

Only a couple of months ago, I had reminded God I was not getting any younger and I would like to enjoy my life before I am done. So much for that dream. It is time to re-examine my life and where I am right now. I need to count my blessings. I am not waiting in a food bank line. I am not a single mother with several children living in a small apartment in New York where the kids can't even get outside or go to the playground. We have an income, we have plenty to eat, and I can go outside or to another room. Compared to so many others, I am so blessed. Although we are to stay away from others, I went to a friend for part of the day. For my own well-being, I just had to get away from him.

My marriage has never been what I had hoped it would be. I can only hope I have learned enough in this lifetime to choose more wisely in my next life. I feel certain I will outlive Dick. Because I have never lived alone, I am not certain how I will feel about living by myself. The days when Dick is cranky, I feel it can't be worse than living with someone who is almost always in a bad mood. It is hard to understand why he can be pleasant when others are around but is a completely different person with me. When he acts like this, I wonder if he feels as poorly as he says, or is it a way of making me feel sorry for him because he supposedly feels so bad? I am never sure how he feels because he has always been a complainer. I often think I bet he wishes he felt as good as he did twenty-five years ago when he began complaining daily.

I have been extremely tired lately. Dick has been having a hard time and has had numerous doctor appointments to which I have been taking him. I have been watching Kailee several days a week and as I am not ready to give up on my flower beds, I have been trying to put mulch down. Our lot comprises more than one acre. I know I have too many flower beds, but I enjoy looking at them and I also enjoy taking care

O Holy Spirit, Enlighten Me

of them when I have the time to do so. Thus far, I have made five trips to the lumber company for mulch and need to go at least one more time. Soon, I will have the flower beds done and that will free up some of my time. I find it relaxing to work outside, so I am not actually complaining about that.

I really wish I could be more positive about Dick, but I have spent my life accepting him as he is and now that I am stuck in the house with him daily, and he is always in a negative mood, I am finding it very hard to continue accepting him as he is. I only recently realized I have never heard my husband tell me to have a good time when I leave or ask if I had a good time when I returned. I have spent my life thinking about my family, then Tina, then my grandkids. It never occurred to me I wasn't really happy. This was just the way my life was and I had accepted it. In my own way, I was as blind as Dick. Today, I almost never leave the house unless it is for something I need. Previously, I could leave and visit my friends when I was getting disgusted with things, but life has changed with the virus.

When I look outside my own life, I realize how many people are in despair at the present time. We are all dealing with an out-of-control virus and people have taken to the streets to protest the unnecessary death of a black man at the hands of the police. We are all witnessing history. The things that are happening today will be read about forever in the history books. Once again, I am fortunate enough to not be experiencing the same despair so many are feeling at this time.

It is June, and I hadn't seen my friends since February but things are slowly opening up and I am looking forward to getting together at one of their homes tomorrow. None of us are ready to go to restaurants.

I. M. Free

The day after I saw my friends, I couldn't believe how uplifting it was just to see them. The isolation has taken a toll on my friends. I could really see a difference in several of them. The time home alone has not been kind to them. I hope we can begin to get together regularly once again. It gives us all something to look forward to. I have been so tired and have been pushing myself to get things done. It was as though a load had been lifted off me just doing something other than my usual routine at home.

Dick has been having a very bad week. He has barely moved all week. I know he doesn't feel well. He had gone to bed at 6:00 PM last night. This morning, he once again is feeling poorly so I made him biscuits and sausage. The lawn needs mowing and because Dick spent the past week moaning after having mowed the lawn, I told him I was going to mow the lawn. Just like New Year's Eve, Dick had an amazing recovery. He insisted he would mow the lawn.

One day, I think Dick is physically done and the next, he is out mowing the lawn. This is why I never truly know how Dick is actually feeling. Trying to figure out how he really feels wears me out. I'm so tired of the games I feel he plays. Once again, I am asking myself, am I being manipulated? I feel like I am and that makes me disgusted with him.

This evening, Dick and I had a shouting match about where to put the mower I use. It would be so simple to put it in Dick's garage which now has two old unusable mowers in it. I wanted him to put one of those in the shed in the back, as it is hard to get my mower into the shed with the mower attachment on it. Dick screamed at me and once again insisted I must always have my way. At this point, Kailee went over and hit Dick in the chest area. Lance got upset with Kailee

O Holy Spirit, Enlighten Me

and scolded her. I pointed out, "She was only defending her Grandma," which was exactly what she was doing. Dick's voice is so ugly when he gets upset. I hate for the grandkids to overhear the ugly conversation that occurs between Dick and me. The honest truth is we do nothing my way without an argument. I really believe this is the devil at work and the devil wants me to feel guilty when Dick is no longer here. I am going to have to keep a positive mind and not let the devil do this to me. I know I give much more than Dick in order to try and keep the peace, but I am getting to the place I would rather just put all of this behind me.

The argument with Dick left me totally exhausted. I am truly ready for my life to change. Each time he gets angry and raises his voice, I feel like I die a little more. I am not ready to leave this life, but I just cannot keep doing this with Dick. I am so ready to move to the next step. I know it is coming, but why does it have to take so long and take me down with it?

All my married life when I spoke up and disagreed with Dick, I have heard the same response, "You have to have everything your way." Only God knows how many times I haven't said anything and how seldom I have disagreed with his decisions. You cannot disagree with Dick on anything. I just don't want to do this any longer. It is time for life to change.

I feel God has been preparing me for some time to live without Dick. He made me get my life in order so I would be ready when I was alone. God then made me look at my marriage as it truly was, made me accept the discontent I felt, and now I feel ready to move on without guilt on my part because the marriage didn't live up to my expectations. You cannot change things alone. Both parties must be willing to accept there is a problem and must be willing to work out

I. M. Free

those problems. Dick has never dealt with anything. He sees everything the way he wants to see it and that is as far as he goes on anything. He has never been able to discuss anything. His mind could not be any more closed than it is.

Dick has always made me feel everything was my fault. God has shown me this is not true. God has explained to me things that I didn't see or chose to overlook. I have always occupied my mind with other things so I wouldn't have to look at the trouble in our marriage. I played tennis until my life became filled with worrying about my parent's and sister's health. After they were gone, my life was consumed with worrying about Tina. After Tina passed, Dick began having one medical problem after another, and I concentrated on my grandkids. Then came the virus, the inability to escape my home life, and the realization I was terribly dissatisfied with my husband and my marriage.

When I went to bed last night, I knew I was ready to let go. The devil will not be able to make me feel guilty about my marriage. I saw so clearly how the only way to get along with Dick is to do absolutely everything his way. I can't do that. I am too tired. I have to be free to be me. The past months have shown me how manipulative and controlling he is. The back porch used to be my haven, where I could go and relax. The porch has now become his place to sit. If I want to go to Melanie's, he goes along. When I go to the store, if I am gone too long, there will be a remark about how long it took me. When I had a video conference with my doctor, he sat on the other end of the couch so he could hear everything that was said. I feel totally smothered and I have no peaceful place to be by myself except in my bedroom. The most relaxed I have felt in months was the afternoon I spent with my school friends. After that visit, I came home and felt I could breathe again. But that feeling didn't last, because the reality of my life set back in. I am ready to let go. I want to let go.

God prepared me for Tina's death and now He has prepared me to live without Dick. Dick doesn't look well and doesn't act like a person that has a long life ahead of him. His mind spends too much time in negative places and there is nothing anyone can do to cure that. It is something only he can change and I am quite certain he doesn't have a clue where to begin. He is who he is and doesn't know how to change anything about himself. He is totally in God's hands. I don't have the inner strength to even discuss things with him any longer. I told God last night I was ready. The devil will not make me feel guilty no matter what happens. I have done my best but it is something that is not in my control.

Whenever I think of Tina, I once again realize how fortunate I am to know she is right here, with me. How can I dwell on the past and feel poorly when I know she is here, happy and healthy? It just makes me love her all the more. I will forever be grateful to God for the knowledge He has given me and the total peace of mind I receive when thinking of death. I would so much rather let go than watch someone suffer. I don't ever want to suffer, so why would I want someone else to suffer? I have a hard time living with the flu for a day or so. I can't imagine days on end of pain and discomfort. I felt I inadvertently caused my mother another year of suffering because I wasn't ready to let her go. I don't want to hold someone here because of my inability to set them free. I believe God gives us the time we need to accept the death of a loved one and sometimes, it takes some of us longer than others to let go.

Chapter 25

When I awakened this morning, I realized how much the past months have pulled me down. Being trapped in my home twenty-four seven with someone with such a negative outlook has changed me. I need to mentally put myself above Dick's problems.

Dick is once again having a really bad day. He could barely get out of the car after we picked up his hearing aids. He has had them refitted three times, as they keep falling out of his ears. He can hardly get around and is totally disoriented. I asked him twice if he wanted to go to the hospital, but he doesn't want to go.

The next day, Kailee was watching television. Dick did his usual thing and was talking to her almost constantly, not allowing her to watch the cartoon. Dick told me later that when I left the room, Kailee told him she didn't care about him. That really hurt him. But as I know how he treated Tina and I know this is Tina's soul reborn, I completely understand where Kailee's remark came from. Later on the

O Holy Spirit, Enlighten Me

way to swimming, I explained she shouldn't talk to Grandpa that way because it hurts his feelings. I want to correct her, but I don't want to make her feel guilty.

Kris called and I told her I had almost called her twice because of her father's health. I told her it is like he is on a roller coaster. One day, he is totally down and then he comes back. It is so tiring. I truly will be surprised if the end is not near. He gets so depressed and his outlook is not positive about anything.

Kris will be home in a couple of weeks. My daughter, son-in-law, two grandkids, their spouses, and four great-grandkids are coming home for a vacation. We haven't all been together for years and we have never seen the two newest great-grandkids. Sometimes, I wonder if Dick will make it until they get here. It is something of which I am never sure. He has ups and he has downs. It seems the downs are definitely following his mowing the lawn. I had planned on mowing the last two times but he has insisted on doing it himself.

After speaking with Kris, I was taking Kailee to my friends to swim. On the way, I dodged a dead possum on the road. Kailee asked me why I did that. I said, "Because, for one thing, I don't want it on my tires." Kailee asked, "What is the number two thing?" I could only laugh at her question. "There is no number two thing."

When we came home, Kailee went next door to play. I called a friend and was talking with her when Dick came out to the back porch. I had the air conditioning running as it was in the eighties and it hadn't been turned on all day. The porch was warm. Dick asked me to turn the air conditioner off. Without thinking, I turned it off and went into the house. Moments later, I asked myself, "Why did I turn the air conditioner off? It was in the eighties." I often listen to him and just automatically do what he says.

I took Kailee home after a day of swimming. Jenna was now home from nursery school. She brought me her shoes, sat down, and held up her foot, meaning she wanted her shoes on. After I put the shoes on, she tried to tell me something I didn't understand. I told her, "Show me what you want." She went to the door leading to the garage and tried to open the door. Lance had just told her she couldn't go outside. I told her, "Ask Daddy if you can go outside." At sixteen months, she firmly answered, "No." She is so smart and cute.

Dick has been withdrawn before and it concerned me, but this time, it definitely feels different. I am sure he is down because of the way Kailee spoke to him the other day, but in my heart, I feel this is nothing more than payback, as it is exactly how he treated Tina. We all wish the world existed without pain, but this is not heaven, and pain seems to play a big part in our growth.

Dick has been extremely quiet the past two days. He has kept his eyes shut the majority of the time. It is like he isn't even here. It feels as though he is at complete peace. He went to bed last night at 6:30 PM. Tonight, it was 5:30 PM.

This is the third day in a row that Dick has slept nearly all day. When he got up, he drove the lawn tractor to the backyard to look at Melanie's garden, the very same tractor I had to fight to get put in his garage versus the shed in the back. He was only gone a very short time, came back in, and went to bed. I wonder if he will make it till the kids get home in a week. He has pulled out of this several times before, will he do it again? He is always cold but has resorted to shorts

O Holy Spirit, Enlighten Me

the last two days. It is very hot outside, still, he covers himself with a blanket.

I feel I am near the end of the road as far as paying for the pain I caused others in my last life. In my previous life, I believe I left my children and family and headed west to care for my father, leaving my oldest child (my mother in this lifetime) the burden of raising her three brothers. I believe I will soon have finished my penance for my poor judgment in a past life and I will begin to enjoy life as I never have previously in this lifetime. This makes so much sense to me and I believe it because it is what my body is telling me. Although I was selfish in my last life, I know I have spent the past forty and some years thinking of others, not myself. I am a better person because of this and today, I am comfortable with who I am.

I continue to feel I am blessed. Even when extremely tired, I do not get depressed. God keeps my spirits up by the little things He does that let me know He is with me and He understands. I have days when I think I just can't take Dick to another doctor's appointment, but when the time comes, God gives me the strength I need to do it. Sometimes, I feel the weight of my cross so heavily I feel exhausted, then God lifts that cross and I find I can make it one more time. Dick has an appointment this morning and another tomorrow morning. The only good thing is they are his appointments, not mine. I have been so blessed with good health all my life. When I see all the people who are suffering, I know how fortunate I am. I continually thank God for my good health.

In my heart, I know one day I am going to enjoy life. It has been a long road, but freedom isn't far away. I have no doubt God will reward me for listening and following Him. Very few people will understand why I have chosen to live my life as I have. I have heard more than once, "Just change it." When you are truly following God, you don't make those changes on your own. You wait for Him to direct you. It is not always an easy thing to do, but it is the right thing to do.

Because of the virus, our lives have changed so much this year. It is suggested that we stay six feet away from others. Some people wear masks, others do not. At the present time, there are no organized professional sports to attend or watch on television. Restaurants are either not open, at half capacity, or open for pickup only. Activities are limited pretty much to your own imagination though some are slowly opening with social distancing. If this virus doesn't cause another shutdown, it will probably be a miracle, as so many people see the entire thing as a hoax. I am not one of them.

Most of the news these days regards politics and the virus, thus I have resorted to listening to music. I listen to anything that is relaxing and puts me in a better place. When my girls were small, I listened to music a lot. Somehow over the years, I got away from listening to music. I think I drifted away from that when I could no longer understand the words being sung. I listen to old music, when you could understand the words and enjoy the message. Today's music is often just noise or words you don't really want to hear.

Yesterday was Dick's 82nd birthday. His cousin, Paula, brought him two meals after bringing him a dozen energy drinks the previous day. It hasn't made a difference in Dick. Although he tells everyone he hasn't slept in days, he continues to be completely drained and is sleeping almost non-stop. The previous times a family member was in their last days, they weren't living under the same roof as me. I could get away from it somewhat, but this is different. There is no place to escape, except to friends for a short visit or a trip to the store for something we need.

Dick has spent most of today moaning as though he is in horrible pain. Melanie called his doctor's office to get the results of the blood test they took a few days ago. He has a low-grade infection. I am wondering tonight if he is actually in horrible pain or if this his usual lack of tolerance to any kind of pain.

I am so tired of his never-ending complaints that I am totally ready to let go. I feel as if I have been his lifelong mental punching bag for everything that isn't perfect in his life. I just do not want to put up with his being totally disagreeable with me about almost everything. Unless you have personally been the target of this type of abuse, you can't possibly understand how it wears you down. I am mentally exhausted from hearing his almost daily complaints about everything I do that isn't exactly the way he would do something. It is as though I am supposed to bow to his every whim and do as he wants. I just want to be free of it. I don't want him to die, but if that is the way it has to be for me to escape, then so be it. It is not my choice; it is God's choice. God knows I have had enough; let Him show me the way out. It really doesn't matter to me, just so there is some sort of change. No matter what, I do not want to spend the rest of my life with Dick. I will never be able to forget the fifty-seven years of verbal abuse. He is so different in front of others; mostly everyone who knows him will not believe how he acts toward me. He is not a pleasant person when it comes to me.

I wish I knew how much pain he actually is in because he has been complaining non-stop for nearly twenty-five years. Kris will be here tomorrow. I wonder how he will feel

I. M. Free

when they get here. Will he have a miraculous recovery or will he still be moaning and complaining in front of them? It amazes me how the moaning stops when he is alone. It seems to only happen when you are in the same room with him or within hearing distance. It makes me doubt how much pain he actually is in. He has cried wolf all of our married life.

When I talked to Kris, she suggested the reason Kailee doesn't want anything to do with Dick is because of the way she has heard him speak to me. The last time he shouted at me in front of her, she had gone over and hit him. That was a couple of weeks ago and Kailee hasn't let him get close to her since. She pretty much ignores him, which is killing Dick, but he brings it on himself with his ugly tone.

Kris and her family will be here for about eight days. I am looking forward to seeing them, but wish I had a little more energy. I suggested everyone stay at Melanie's, as I am honestly not up to taking care of anyone else at the present time, and it will be more relaxing for Dick if no one is staying here and he feels he needs to stay awake. Although most everyone discourages travel with the virus presently out of control in many states, I believe perhaps it is God's will they come home at this time.

My brother won't be joining us, as he prefers to remain isolated because of the virus. I went to see him to make sure he was okay, as he hasn't been feeling well. He was angry at the Veterans, which gave him extra adrenaline. He will be fine.

We are expecting the family to arrive from Louisiana this evening. The kids all want pizza when they get here and Dick no longer likes to eat pizza. I made Dick a steak, corn on the cob, and baked sweet potato so that he would have the

O Holy Spirit, Enlighten Me

strength to get through this evening. He usually is only good for one meal a day anyway.

When the family got here, it was great to be together again. Everyone is doing well and the three little ones are almost all the same size. A short time after they arrived, Dan ordered the pizza for everyone as it had been a long day and they were hungry. That is their usual thing to do when they get here, order their favorite pizza. They will have pizza again while here and usually take some home when they leave. Dick had given me $100 and told me to pay for the pizza. I put the money on the window sill in the kitchen and told Dan to take the money, but he didn't take the money. He took care of it himself.

After a beautiful enjoyable evening, the younger family members went to Melanie's and Kris and Dan went to the room they had reserved.

The next morning, the first thing on Dick's mind is, "Who paid for the pizza?" I told him, "Dan paid for it. I had told him the money was on the window sill, but he didn't pick it up." I told Dick, "You can pay for another meal." The next thing out of Dick's mouth was, "Where is the money I had in my bedroom?" Dick had over one thousand dollars under the dresser scarf in his bedroom. I answered, "I put it in the lockbox." Dick's reply was, "I want to stop the direct payment of checks to the bank. I don't like it that way." I answered, "I can see you are feeling better. We are back on your money. It isn't our money. It is your money." I screamed at him, "This has been the problem in our entire marriage. It has never been our money. It is your money." He was sitting on the porch, wrapped in his blanket. I ignored him, and once again went into the house and slammed the door. I called my friend and released the anger I was feeling. After I got off the phone, I took the money out of the lockbox and threw it at Dick. I yelled at him, "Your obsession with money has ruined our entire marriage." I feel he is so sick in his mind when it comes to money. I am totally fed up with him. I just want to get away from him. I had several thousand dollars in my hand and threw it at him. I shouted, "Take this money and shove it up your butt." It floated over him to the floor. He screamed at me, "Pick that up." I ignored him and once again slammed the door and went back into the house. Let him pick it up.

Dick is so manipulative he thinks everyone plays the head games he plays. I don't play games and I am not withholding his stinking money from him. Except for the home equity loan that he knows nothing about, I have never hidden money from him. I will always feel the home equity loan was not something I did for myself, but something I did for God. I would have taken a vacation had I been doing it for myself. When I had to take out that loan, I told God, "I did this for you. You better cover my butt." And thus far, He has. The payments for the loan are less than $100 a month. It isn't a large loan, but I absolutely hate to owe money.

I have never been obsessed with the acquisition of money, as Dick has been. It is so important to him that it has controlled his entire life. There are so many things we haven't done because he didn't want to spend the money. He has no problem spending money on himself, but if it includes his family, he has a different attitude. I have asked myself so many times why I stayed with him and tolerate the lifestyle he has imposed on me. I know I am a good person.

I have bought things and not told him about it, but it was never anything expensive or outlandish. It was the way I had to live in order to enjoy something I really wanted or felt I needed. I know my life wouldn't have been any easier if I had left him. He is very vindictive and he would have made me pay one way or another. Of that I am certain.

I have often thought people don't actually know you unless they live with you. Dick appears to be a good, generous, and likable person. Behind closed doors, he is a completely different person. It is hard to believe one person can have two such different personalities. In his mind, I am the enemy. He has always had the attitude that I am supposed to do what he wants me to do. He has never accepted I have a mind of my own. I don't owe it to him to do everything his way. I have tried very hard to get along with him. I relent over and over again in order to keep the peace. The one time I don't do it his way, I get screamed at and told over and over again, "We have to do everything your way." That is so very untrue.

When Dick acts like he did this morning, I feel it is the devil after my soul. The devil would love for me to say or do something for which I will be unable to forgive myself after Dick is gone. The devil doesn't like the things I say and do. He doesn't want people to understand life after death. He wants us to be sad and mourn. God wants us to understand all is not lost. Death is not the end. It is a new beginning. I truly believe when our soul leaves our body, we understand everything. We hear and know what others are saying or feeling about us. The departed soul isn't revengeful, but forgiving and understanding. The departed soul will be trying to lead us in a positive direction, trying to make us a better person. This is what the departed soul will do until they are once again reborn and enter a new body where they will continue their own journey at becoming the person deserving of going to heaven.

I. M. Free

I know I am not without sin. My phone has been disconnected three times in the past two weeks when I was saying something negative about others. It is God reminding me I am not perfect and I need to be less judgmental and more understanding of others. This is something I need to work a little harder on. I am well aware I am not perfect. God never hesitates to let me know that. I am just grateful God is understanding and forgiving of my faults.

Chapter 26

The kids came to the house. The family ordered lunch from a local restaurant and after everyone had eaten, we relaxed on the back porch. There are three one-year-olds on the floor. Two can walk, one cannot. Jenna reached over, pulled Bryce to her, and planted a kiss on his face. Bryce in turn put his arm around Jena, pulled her to him, and planted a kiss on her. It was the most beautiful moment I could remember in a very long time. It will probably never happen again and unfortunately, no one got it on video. When I told my grandson about it later, I said, "I wonder if they recognized one another."

Brayton, the seven-year-old, is riding Kailee's motorized scooter in the backyard. He has his one-year-old brother standing between his legs on the scooter. Bryce is loving it and has a big smile on his face. It is not something I would have done, but this is a different generation and his parents didn't seem to think anything of it—another precious moment that I did not catch on video.

I. M. Free

Today, the Louisiana family has gone to Put-in-Bay for a couple of days. Dick is not getting any stronger and is finding it hard to eat anything. He is becoming extremely thin and is still having problems with an infection. He seems to be delirious and I know he is very weak.

Two days later, the family has returned from Put-in-Bay. Shane and his family have gone to Pennsylvania to see his wife's family, but the rest of the family came to the house this afternoon. Dick is having a really bad day. He appears extremely weak and disoriented. After the family left, I told Melanie I didn't want to be home alone with him tonight. I was actually afraid he might be gone by morning. As Dick wouldn't voluntarily go to the hospital, Melanie and I decided perhaps we should have the paramedics come and check him. The paramedics came, checked him, and told him he was a very sick man. They convinced him to go to the hospital.

Because of the coronavirus, only one person is allowed to visit Dick at the hospital, thus Melanie is the person who will be attending Dick. I am exhausted and haven't left the couch all day. The arguments with Dick over petty things, the excessive heat, and his unwillingness to go to the hospital have certainly taken a toll on me. It was 90 degrees on our porch. We hadn't turned on the air conditioner as Dick is always cold and wrapped in either a blanket or wearing a fleece jacket. I am certain Dick and I are both dehydrated from being on the porch all day yesterday.

As Melanie is tending her father at the hospital, I am home with the kids. Yesterday, Melanie and Kris were playing with one of the kid's toys. They would spell bad words and the toy would giggle. Today, Kailee asked me to tell her a bad word. "I am not going to tell you a bad word." She pleaded several times for me to tell her a bad word. I responded, "I wouldn't be a very good grandma if I told you bad words. What would Meme (her other grandmother) think if I told you bad words?" Once again, I am amazed at Kailee's awareness of what is going on around her. She often is listening and absorbing, even when the conversations don't include her.

The family has been socializing like there isn't a contagious virus around, which is exactly why we are having record-breaking numbers of new cases every day. The way you feel about the virus is directly related to your political beliefs and the station you listen to on television. Some feel it is just the flu and nothing to be concerned about; others would like to try and contain the virus. Some wear masks, others do not. I do wear a mask and I try to be cautious about where I go and keep away from crowds. I really wish the family took it a little more seriously.

This morning, I told Melanie to tell the family I just want to be alone today. Dick is in the hospital and I don't have the energy to get together. I feel bad because they will only be here for a few days. It will be quite a while until I see them again, but I am completely exhausted. I want the family to enjoy themselves while they are here. So, while I sat at home, the family went to a local amusement park for the kids and are doing their own thing today.

Dick called from the hospital and wanted to know why he was there. He obviously couldn't remember the previous days. I told him he was there because he is bleeding and they are trying to find out why. The nurse got on the phone and said he was confused and very different. She asked, "Was that something they should be concerned about?" I sort of laughed and said, "I know that person." Dick can be so pleasant one day and so nasty the next. I assumed his ugly side came out and she wanted to know if this was something new. I told her he was confused when he came in.

The family is leaving tomorrow but today again, I am too exhausted to even want to see them. They all went in different directions and caught up with old acquaintances.

When I think of Dick, there is nothing more to say. I don't have a thing left I want to say to him. I am trying to remember when I received a word of appreciation, a compliment, an encouragement, a kind word, a thank you, or some understanding from him of what my life has been like.

I don't know what more I could have done. I haven't been able to say I love him since I was pregnant with Melanie and he didn't speak to me during the entire pregnancy. What little love that was left at that time disappeared during those months. It was then I really saw the man to whom I was married, and I didn't like him very much, but even so, I stayed and continued to do the best I could. I forgave him, but I never respected him as a person after that.

I am concerned in a day or so Melanie is going to be as exhausted as me. Hopefully, by that time, I will have some strength back and can take over for her with the kids. I haven't been this exhausted for a long time. I can only hope I bounce back quickly, like tomorrow. I've been sitting on my couch for two days and I am feeling a little better this evening. My energy is beginning to come back. I can't help but wonder what tomorrow has in store.

I hadn't seen the family for two days, but my grandson, Shane, came over this evening and we had a nice talk. He doesn't seem to enjoy the same financial freedom the rest of his family enjoys. He is so like my dad in many ways. He is a good kid. I just hope he finds the right job that will keep his interest and motivate him. He deserves to be successful. He is a hard worker and a good person.

I slept well last night but I am still exhausted. I feel like I have been carrying Dick for the past three years and I just can't carry both of us any longer. I don't have the energy to look out for him right now. He is pulling me down and I don't want to be pulled down. I have a headache and am sick to my stomach. I just want to relax and not think about feeding and cleaning up after Dick. He doesn't do anything at all for himself. He leaves the bathroom an ungodly mess and I have to clean it regularly. In his entire life, he has never been able to see the mess he makes and clean up after himself. I would like to enjoy my life for a while before my time is up.

In all honesty, the only thing Dick has done for the past three years is occasionally mowing the lawn and hang the storm door and I wasn't happy about the way that was done. He never has helped around the house. He has always done his own thing which was usually to build something in his garage or go hunting.

There are two publishing companies interested in discussing my book. I am to contact them at the beginning of next week after the family returns to Louisiana. I have a feeling something good will come of one of the contacts. I will listen to God and make a decision accordingly.

Chapter 27

Before Kris left, I told her, "I don't want to hurt your father, but I honestly just can't take any more." Kris got tears in her eye and didn't say anything. I told her I think Dick should have married someone who was not as strong as me—someone who would make him feel really important and needed. I was not that person. I told her I feel he has always been trying to break me, and I wouldn't be broken. I am not broken now, but I have gone as far as I can with him. If I stayed with him, sooner or later, I, like two of my friends, will also have a heart attack. I hope I am smart enough not to let that happen. I have to get away to save myself. This is what will allow me to give up on my marriage and not feel guilty about quitting. There truly is nothing more I can give this marriage. God is letting me go.

When I woke up this morning, I knew I had been letting go of Dick for the past week. My body is telling me I can't continue to live with him. My breathing is deep and labored. I can let go and know I gave him all I had to give.

O Holy Spirit, Enlighten Me

The thought of continuing to argue with him over ridiculous things is truly taking my life away. I have to get away and set myself free from his domineering control of me.

I will continue to listen to God and follow Him every day, but I just can't continue on the road I have been on with Dick for all these years. It wouldn't matter if he changed. It is too late. There are too many things I can no longer block out. I don't want to. He has made no attempt to get stronger and hasn't changed his bullheaded mindset. I want to be free from all of it. I want to let go and move forward.

Most of Dick's friends think he is wonderful. To the outside world, he is a happy, pleasant person, but that is not the man I live with. To me, Dick is usually depressed, negative, controlling, demanding, cheap, and selfish, all of which he hides extremely well from the rest of the world. I really don't want to spend the rest of my life with him. It is time for me to gather my strength and change my life.

I have been short of breath, especially when I talk or walk. I have shortness of breath, a slight cough, headache, aching legs, and occasional discomfort in my chest. I want to mark it up to stress, but Melanie insists I get tested. I know she is right. I don't want to have something and unknowingly spread it around. I called my doctor's office and they have arranged for me to have a COVID-19 test.

This morning, Melanie took me to the hospital where a nurse came to the car and stuck a swab up my nose. I still believe it is just stress, but in a day or so, I will know for sure.

It takes me forever to just find the energy to put my thoughts into the computer. This has left my mind unable to focus for longer than a few minutes. I hate feeling this way. There are so many things I would like to be physically fit to do. I have delayed making a couple of important phone calls. I can't even make myself do that. Talking takes my breath away and my throat becomes irritated. I haven't been this exhausted since I was dealing with hypoglycemia. It is very similar. I have to concentrate on getting my strength back. I have done nothing but sit on my butt for eight days. I only get up to eat or go to the bathroom. Although I'd like to be working on my book, I can't even watch the television or do a puzzle. I know when it is time my strength will return and I will be able to focus.

I hadn't talked to Dick since he called and asked why he was in the hospital. I have spent the past days thinking about my life and where I am. Dick has left the hospital and is now in rehab. He called and asked, "Babe, are you mad?" I calmly answered, "I am done with you, period. I don't have anything to say to you," and calmly hung up the phone. I didn't feel bad about what I did. I wasn't angry. I was too exhausted to care.

If Dick had treated me better the past fifty-seven years, I could have gotten through this, but he has been so unpleasant to live with and has never shown any appreciation to whatever I have tried to do for all of us. The latest arguments were the last straw in what has been a very dissatisfying marriage. On the positive side, I know I am much wiser than I was when I married him and will never let anyone do this to me again. I think one thing I will take into my next life is not taking on more than I can financially afford to support on my own. I was trapped in this marriage, just as my mother was trapped in her marriage. I now understand why my mother let my father abuse her as he did. She had no other choice if she wanted to be with her children.

O Holy Spirit, Enlighten Me

I am trying to relax, but my breathing is so heavy. My mind is remembering the many times I tried to talk to Dick. There was no way to communicate with him. His mind was closed to almost anything I said because, in his mind, I was trying to tell him what to do. He has been this way almost from the beginning.

Because Dick is in a rehab facility, I truly believe God is giving me the time to let go. I can let go because my body is telling me to let go. I keep remembering my friend of more than sixty-five years who passed away nearly two years ago of a massive heart attack. Her marriage was so comparable to mine.

I received a phone call from a social worker at the rehab facility. She asked if the three of us (meaning Dick, myself, and she) could discuss this. I said, "No." She asked if I thought Dick could take care of himself. I said to her, "He hasn't done a thing for three years, what do you think?"

I am asking God, "Do I really need to do this? I don't really want to. What makes me think it would ever occur to him he wasn't perfect? In fifty-seven years, he has never accepted any responsibility for anything in our marriage. Why would he think he was the problem now? I am not angry at him. I don't need an apology from him. Nothing he could say would make a difference. It is over. If he has regrets, it is too late. I don't need to rehash any of it with him.

This evening, I am beginning to feel better. My breathing is much better. I think telling Dick I was through with him has taken a heavy burden off me. I am not sorry about what I said or did. I love my porch and backyard. That is where I find peace with God because it is so quiet and peaceful. If giving it up is the price I have to pay for my life, then I guess it is just a price I will have to pay. I have believed for some time Dick was going to pass away, but I realize he could finally decide he wants to live and get his life together. Either way, in my heart, I know I am doing what I need to do for me. Dick is in God's hands, not mine. I will continue to take life one day at a time and follow where God leads me.

Because I don't have the energy to do much else, I think about my marriage and how it got me to where I am now. It never mattered what I wanted. Dick's response had always been the same, "You don't need it." After nearly forty years of that, I learned to just go get what I wanted, knowing I was going to pay for it with a verbal outburst, followed by silence. I have learned to live with that also.

Since he has been laid up for months, I started going through his possessions in the basement and garage. Things I had never been allowed to move. When I saw the prices of some of the things he owned, I began to see what a fool I had been. He made me feel guilty about everything I ever purchased, even though those purchases more often than not were for the entire family to enjoy. When I found he had nearly two thousand dollars hidden in the garage, I began to understand why he didn't want me in the garage. He has spent a lifetime accusing me of hiding his money.

He has never had a problem looking me in the eye and lying. I am beginning to find out about many of those lies. It only helps to set me free. I am not angry about it. I am just glad God has shown me exactly the type of person I married. I feel so sorry for him. In my opinion, he is a lost soul, but I know it is no longer up to me to help him. He must do it himself. I am just grateful God has made me see the light. It makes life so much easier for me to accept, knowing I did my best and I am now pretty much finished with that chapter of my life. I know the future is going to be hard, but I feel I am ready to face it.

If someone walks out on a marriage too soon, there will always be questions, "Did I do the right thing?" I stayed until I knew God was setting me free. It isn't how I wanted my life to be, but I truly believe it was probably the life I deserved. I believe I previously caused others a lot of pain and grief because of my own selfishness. For this, I had a price to pay, and I believe I have now paid that price. I believe God has good things in store for me and I am looking forward to enjoying that life. I just want to live in peace and feel good about myself.

Jenna had run a fever for a few days after the family left, and Melanie's doctor suggested Jenna be tested. Jenna's virus test came back negative, just as I am sure mine will be on Monday. Dick had gone to the rehab facility while I awaited the results of my COVID-19 test. This morning, Melanie and Lance took the girls to see Grandpa through the plastic shield at rehab. On the way home, Melanie stopped in with the girls. I was happy to see them. When they left, Jenna closed her eyes, wrinkled her nose, and had the cutest smile on her face.

Melanie suggested Dick go to her house when he leaves the rehab facility, as he will have several follow-up doctor appointments in the coming week. It would be easier for her if he was already at her house. She told him he really couldn't be around me until I got the results of the virus test. As it turned out, I didn't get the results for five days, which gave me more time to think about what to do. As his last appointments were Friday, she told him she would take him home after that.

He agreed to go to her house. He could spend time with the grandkids.

My mind keeps wandering back to the past and the road Dick and I have been on. I have no regrets on my part. I know I did my best. I wanted to quit numerous times, but my conscience would never let me. Dick has not been easy to live with.

Sometimes, we will have periods when we need someone to help us, but it seems Dick has made a career of it. He hasn't tried to get stronger. It seems he concentrates on being sick and has found something to keep him down time after time. You must want to get better. You need to exercise in some manner to keep up your strength. Dick did nothing. He sat in a chair and slept most of the day. His body is so out of shape that just walking to his garage isn't easy to do. If you sit and think I'm sick or I hurt, day after day, year after year, you are going to be sick and you are going to hurt. That is what you are telling your mind. You must tell yourself, "I want to get better, I want to feel better, I can do this." The mind and body respond to our messages.

Dick is supposed to leave the rehab hospital this morning. I talked with Melanie and I told her I am not angry at Dick. I am not doing what I am doing out of vengeance. My body feels as though I am carrying the weight of the world when I even think of speaking to Dick. My heart rate rises and my breathing gets heavier. I know I am not supposed to talk with him. I feel sorry for him and I am totally aware he is a lost soul. Although I knew he had not passed, my body felt as though he had. I don't know what God has planned but we all feel what we feel for a reason. We all have lessons to learn. I am totally aware I also have lessons to learn, but I have learned to listen to my body and make decisions accordingly. I am so grateful to God for the things I feel. He truly does prepare me for things and for that, I will forever be grateful. Truthfully, I hope all of this passes rather quickly.

I thought to myself, please do not call me, Dick. I really can't take any more. I know I was not perfect. Nothing can erase the past. It was the way it was and we both have to live with that. I thought, how ironic. I am reliving my mother's last days with my father. When she was done, she was done. She never spoke of him after their last argument and didn't even care to hear about his funeral.

As I don't have the energy to do anything else, I continue to spend time thinking about my marriage and what went wrong. Dick never wanted a wife. He wanted someone to take his mother's place. Anything I was capable of doing became my job. He never offered to assist me in any way. He has absolutely no idea how much our vehicle insurance, homeowner insurance, taxes, or utility bills are. He only knows how much money we have in the bank. To him, that was the only important thing.

I don't know if we ever said I love you once we were married. From the beginning, Dick wouldn't talk to me and didn't want to hear what was going on in my mind or world. He was a free spirit, doing as he wanted the majority of the time. He took a set amount of his check every pay and that was his alone. He occasionally paid for dinner when we went out, but just as often, it came out of the money I had on me. I don't recall ever sitting down with Dick and having a conversation regarding anything. Although he does talk to a few of our friends, he wasn't a talker when it came to me. His mind has been so closed our entire marriage. What conversations I had with him usually fell on deaf ears and he would claim I never told him something.

If there is a way to enter a closed mind, I have yet to figure it out. I have a friend who mirrors him. It is hard to have a conversation with her because before you finish your sentence, she is talking about something concerning her. Lately, I have tried to avoid her. It is like the two of them are somewhere else. They don't listen to you. They only want you to listen to them. The only time Dick talked was to complain about his health and how badly he felt. Lately, he has stopped complaining constantly. He just sleeps.

I can't remember when I last enjoyed being around Dick. I don't have any memories of happy times with him. All I have been able to see for years is how unhappy I am being married to him. I have wanted to be free for years. But I was aware God wasn't done teaching me what I needed to learn. I got married too young. When I married, I didn't know myself or what I really wanted, but I have never regretted being a mother. That was what I wanted and I did the best I could. I will never regret becoming a mother.

Chapter 28

My mind keeps rehashing the past. I keep remembering all the times I was accused of spending Dick's money. It is so ironic that I find he is the one hiding money from me. I can't believe how many expensive toys he has bought for himself during our marriage. Toys that in many instances I was told were given to him. I never paid any attention to what he purchased for himself, as I was too busy thinking about family members or paying bills. If it weren't so sad, it would be funny. I just feel sorry for him, as I believe he has a sick mind. How could I live with someone for so long and never have known him? I was so busy defending myself, I didn't look at what he was doing. I guess I never really cared what he was doing. I had let go of him emotionally a long time ago. I can't help but wonder what the next few days have in store because I have no intention of staying in this house with him. I have lined up several friends I can stay with for a night. I don't want to wear my welcome out with anyone. God will guide me when it is time.

I had a bad day yesterday. I was beginning to feel my ability to feel future events was more a curse than a blessing. Once again this morning, I felt Dick's death. I am so tired of feeling this. This is getting harder to live with. I felt exhausted once again and sat on my butt and did a puzzle all day. By this evening, the devil is knocking on my door. Paula called and she too has been feeling poorly for days. Another friend called and I told her of my frustration with my life.

I went for a short drive just to get out. When I returned, I screamed at God about how tired I was of my life and how long this has dragged on. I threw a water bottle and was cleaning up the water when Melanie called with an update. I went to bed. I hate my life and so want it to change.

The next day, I received another phone call from someone interested in representing my book. I didn't pick up the phone and she left a message. It is like I am stuck in my life right now and don't feel I can escape. I again thought about running off to Lake Erie but thought better of it as the last time I tried to escape, my car broke down and it cost me thousands. I don't want to do that again. I just have to remain patient, although it is getting very hard to do. At least, I have lunch with my friends tomorrow and will get out of here.

I have neglected so many things in the past weeks. The lawn needs mowing, but I am just too exhausted to worry about mowing the lawn right now. With a little help, I found someone to take care of that. That was one less thing I needed to worry about. There are so many things I would like to tackle around the house, but I know now is not the time to worry about those things. I need to get my strength back, as I worry sooner or later, Melanie is going to crash. I could hear the tiredness in her voice last night when I talked to her. I told

O Holy Spirit, Enlighten Me

her I would be ready to watch the kids when she needs me. I just know God will give me the strength when I need it.

Today, I met my friends for lunch at an outdoor restaurant. It was so good to get out of my house and be with people I could talk and joke with for a little while. One of my friends is dealing with much of the same situation right now as far as her husband's health. After lunch, I went with a friend and we talked. I accompanied her to a toy store, and afterward, we stopped and got ice cream cones.

When I returned home, I felt as though a weight had been lifted off my chest. I could take deep breaths. I hope that doesn't go away. I hope I am over the hill and can start to relax and truly get my strength back. My friend suggested getting something to help me deal with this, but I told her I like to know I can handle things on my own without taking something. She said she was the same way when she went through her hard times. I feel God is not going to let me die, as I know He wants me to share my story. I am certain there are many women living in similar situations. I just keep on telling Melanie and myself, take it one day at a time. I don't have any other choice at the present time.

Melanie stopped in after picking up Dick's newest prescriptions. When she told me of his upcoming doctor's appointments, it exhausted me just hearing about them. I positively cannot do this much longer. It has been like being married to a child all my life. There is so much Dick doesn't see or understand. It seems he is locked inside his own brain and never sought to get out. I just don't want to be around that environment with him any longer. It is truly like living with a dead man.

Kris called last night. She said when she talked with Dick, he had shown no remorse. He doesn't realize what an imposition it has been on Melanie to take care of him, the kids, her job, and her home. Melanie mentioned he was complaining about money to Kris. Among other things, I guess he is not happy about my paying someone to mow the lawn.

The next day, I again went for a drive just to get away. I was afraid Dick would call and I really didn't want to hear his voice. I think a lot while I am driving. I was remembering the times Dick told me what a good husband he was because he did everything for me. My response was always, "God, I wish you were as wonderful as you think you are." Because Dick earned the money that paid for the roof over our head, in his mind, that made him a good husband. There was nothing more. That was all he needed to do to be a good husband. I guarantee he has never asked himself what more he could have done. Why should he? I made it entirely too easy for him in everything he did. As I drove, I was beginning to do what I always have done, question myself as to whether I could have done more. I thought, maybe I am being too hard on him. Then, the phone rang. It was Melanie. She is already having a dispute with her father over an upcoming doctor's appointment. It brought me back to reality very quickly. I responded, "With Dick, it is always his way, his time, his convenience. I knew it was God bringing me back to reality. I tend to always tell myself I could have done more. That is what I have done to myself all during my marriage. I have always been ready to take more than my share of the blame that we have such a lousy marriage. Then, I remembered the past ten days and how completely exhausted I was and still am. I am feeling stronger and I want to keep getting stronger. The last thing I need right now is Dick upsetting me and putting myself back where I was. I told Melanie I was afraid Dick might call. She said, "Just don't answer the phone."

It has been nearly three weeks since Dick was taken to the hospital. He is supposed to come home tomorrow. The thought of it stresses me. I have a suitcase packed because I don't intend to be here when he gets here. I will just have to take life day by day till I figure out what to do. My breathing becomes labored when I think of being around him. It is something I can't control. I don't even want to hear the sound of his voice.

I know God has a plan. I just don't know right now what that plan is. I positively do not want to be with Dick any longer. I have to move on for my own health. I truly believe one more harsh word between the two of us could be the end of me. That is how tired I am of our relationship and the constant bickering. My breathing is telling me how stressed I am. Some people may be totally unaware of their body giving them messages, but I hear my body and I try very hard to understand what it is telling me.

Dick has two appointments this morning. Melanie will be returning him to our home at about 1:00 PM so I will be out of there before that. Melanie wants me to go to her house to talk, but I will not be bunking at Melanie's this weekend. I have about four options where I could go or I may get a room somewhere. God just hasn't told me what I am going to do. God never makes it easy for me. I wonder, "How often do I have to be tested? It is getting very old." I told Melanie to tell Dick I wouldn't be there when he got home. I'm sure he doesn't believe her, but when she brought him home, I had left. I took my clothes and ended up at my brother's for the night.

Bud has emphysema and is having a really hard time breathing. He told me he wasn't sure he was going to make it the previous night. The weather is very hot and humid and it makes it harder for him to breathe. During our conversation, as he was taking a breathing treatment and smoking his cigarette he said, "This is because of all the drywall dust I breathed." I immediately got a smirk on my face. He saw it and added, "And these cigarettes." Bud and I spent the evening talking about our crappy childhood.

Bud left his bedroom television on all night and the kitchen light is on for a night light. The couch isn't that comfortable, and I can't really stretch out. It was a long night. Unsure my lungs would ever be the same, I couldn't sleep a wink. I said to God, "You better take care of my lungs."

In the morning I understood why I was supposed to be at Bud's. His breathing was terrible. He was gasping for air. I was surprised when I felt no ill effects from sleeping in his smoke-filled apartment. Usually, I would feel discomfort after a short visit. I know Bud isn't going to live to be old, something he knows also. He said his friend wanted him to go to the hospital. He answered, "Why? They can't do anything for me except give me oxygen and a big hospital bill."

It was going to be very hard for Bud to breathe all week. The weather was going to be very hot and humid, so I told him I would go get his groceries. After that, I was not certain where or what I was going to do.

I left Bud's and visited a friend. I told her I wasn't sure where I was going to go that night. I didn't want to put anyone out. About 3:00 PM, after I left her house, I knew where I was to go. I went to the friend I had been avoiding, as she is so much like my husband. At her house, I received a text from another friend that I could spend the night at her house. I had tried to notify her the previous night but she didn't get the message in time. I told her that was fine, but I knew I was supposed to be at my brother's the previous night. I knew Bud's time was limited and it made him feel good that I needed him and things were good between us.

Bud and I had an unfortunate encounter years ago and although we talked, there was always an unspoken distance between us. I felt I needed to go to Bud's so he would know I had let go of the past.

Now at home alone, Dick is angry and told the kids he thinks I am doing this out of spite. He couldn't be more wrong. Days later, Melanie told him, "No, she is doing this to save herself. It came down to you or her, and she decided to save herself."

I really don't like the idea of imposing on my friends. I would rather go to Lake Erie by myself, but I know that is not what I am supposed to do. I again remembered when I decided I needed to get away before Dick's last surgery, and what that trip cost me. I have to wait until I know in my body that it is okay for me to get away. I absolutely hate the idea of Melanie being stuck with taking care of all Dick's needs. She is already too busy with her kids and job. God will tell me what to do when the time comes.

I can't even remember when I last enjoyed being around Dick. It would be more than forty-five years, for sure. It is unbelievable to me that I have stayed and endured his constant disapproval of me and my life choices. I can't remember when he had something positive to say to me or about me. But, truthfully, I don't like him any better.

Many, many years ago, my mother had said to me that life on earth is hell. I am beginning to see what she means. My life has never been easy, and I keep waiting for it to get better. I, like my mother, have decided we are living in hell. While there are many good people on earth, there is an overabundance of lost souls on earth. These people never think much beyond themselves and will do almost anything to get what they want.

It is Sunday morning and my friend and I are going to go out to breakfast. Except for pickup and eating outdoors, I have not eaten inside a restaurant since March. It is the middle of July. I used to eat out regularly. My life has certainly changed.

I think about Dick a little and only feel sorry for him. I am not angry at him. I know he can't help the way he is. It is who he is and I accepted his imperfections a long time ago. His mind is so closed and stuck, how can I feel anything other than pity? I just can't live any longer with the constant verbal attacks, complaints, and worry about money, which we don't actually need to worry about. There are many people who are better off but just as many who don't have the security we do have. He just has never been able to see it and enjoy life.

Chapter 29

Each night I spent with my friends I asked myself, "Why am I here?" "How long am I going to be here?" I would spend two weeks at her home. I knew this was only a temporary fix to my present circumstances. I didn't miss my husband one bit. I actually don't have any emotion left when it concerns him.

While at her home I would get caught up with my current book. Something I couldn't find the time or peace of mind to work on at home. Was that why I was there?

My friend's internet hadn't worked for the past week. I wanted to get in touch with a couple of publishers who were interested in speaking to me regarding my first book, but in my heart, I knew it was not time. With no internet, I had a very good reason to believe it just wasn't time. I was working on this current book and I had no idea how God was going to have me finish it.

At the end of the two-week period, I knew it was time to once again face my life. I knew I needed to go home and face Dick. I really did not want to do that. I feel I could live the rest of my life, never see him again, and have no regrets.

I left my friends, went to my daughter's house, and worked on the previous chapter. I tried to get in touch with a couple of friends but didn't make contact. I was stalling, and I knew it. Not ready to go home I went to a store I like to visit. I didn't buy anything. I just looked. After I left, I once again tried another friend who lived in the area. She too wasn't available.

I decided I was to go to my brother's. On the way, the friend I had just called returned my call and was sorry she missed my call. I told her I would catch up with her later. I felt I was supposed to go to my brothers.

I am glad I went to see Bud. He again is having a really hard time breathing. He was going to contact the veterans next week to see about getting oxygen. Something they should have provided a couple of years ago. He had told me they wanted him to go to the veteran's hospital to take a test to prove he needed the oxygen. He had told them he couldn't be away from his breathing treatments long enough to make the trip. Thus, he has never had oxygen. Something my father had no problem receiving when he needed it.

I left Bud's, went to Melanie's to pick up my computer, and drudgingly headed to my home. When I opened the garage door, the junk tractors that were in Dick's garage were now in my garage. I went into the house and went directly to my room without even glancing at Dick.

Shortly thereafter, he stuck his head in the door and asked, "Don't you want to talk?" I answered, "No, I only came home because I knew it was time to leave my friends." He closed the door and that was all that was said.

The next morning, the first thing I felt was how much Dick's total indifference to me all these years had hurt me. Because I seldom thought about myself, I unbelievably had never dealt with that hurt. I put the hurt out of my mind and knew I had taken one more step toward letting go of my marriage and my husband.

Melanie has let me know I won't have to deal with any more of Dick's doctor appointments or medicines. She was going to take over. I can't say how much that means to me, as I truly cannot deal with his medical problems any longer. For a change, I want to think about myself and what I want from life.

I pray I can live under the same roof with him and not let him pull me into another argument. If he pursues that path with me, I know I will leave immediately and never look back.

God has made me feel his death so often that I believe my body has totally accepted his passing and when the time comes, I will have no regrets. I truly did my best and gave it all I had.

With God, I have learned to live one day at a time. We never know for certain what tomorrow will bring, but if we are truly following God, we know it will be the way it is supposed to be.

Chapter 30

By the time I returned home, I knew it was time to send my latest transcript to a publishing company. At the time two publishing companies were interested in speaking to me about "I Don't Have Time." I e-mailed the second publisher whom had been contacting me and told them I felt God was guiding me in another direction. I didn't ask about or listen to their offer.

I contacted the other publisher and I immediately felt comfortable with the person to whom I was speaking. When originally contacted they were interested in re-releasing my book. But I felt God wasn't ready and requested they change the name of the book and also add the new transcript. I felt I was asking a lot, but I also felt this was what I was to do. Thus I forwarded my transcript and once again turned my life over to God. I had no idea how God was going to have me end my story, but I didn't worry or dwell on that. I have been listening long enough to know I won't know until God is ready for me to know.

O Holy Spirit, Enlighten Me

The month away from Dick helped my nerves. I returned home, although I would have rather not return. But as I always try to follow God's guidance, I knew that was what I was to do. I found that looking at my marriage as it truly was helped to set me even freer than I felt before. I realized I had been avoiding the truth about my life. I was not happy and I needed to figure out exactly why I was not happy. So much of that unhappiness came from my husband. I love my children, my friends, and my house. Only my husband was disappointing me.

I remembered God's message of trying to accept Dick as he was and not let it upset me. It was going to take considerable time, but I knew God was telling me this for my own good. I must have peace of mind in order to live peacefully within myself. I am not a person who can strongly disagree with someone and still have the ability to communicate with God. In order to communicate, I must be at peace and as that is the most important thing in my life, I try very hard to maintain that peaceful feeling.

Dick obviously did some thinking while I was gone because he decided it was time to sell some of the tools in his garage. He hadn't been able to use many of them for years. It was something with which I didn't want to burden our children. I had gone through many of my belongings before I left.

While Dick received a considerable amount of cash for his tools, he refused to put the money in the bank. It is obvious the trust between us is completely gone. It irritates me that he always has this attitude about money. It is who he is, and I realize he isn't going to change. He had my daughter check the balance of our savings account numerous times while I was gone. I hadn't taken a dime out of our account.

I. M. Free

Weeks later Dick needed brakes on his truck. He asked me to get $400 out of the bank. He has a huge amount of money in the house, but I am to get money out of the bank for the brakes. Knowing very well he had more money than he will spend the rest of his lifetime, I said to him, "Getting a little short on cash, are you?" He ignored my comment. I couldn't believe he was that ignorant. God has told me not to let him upset me. It was sometimes a real challenge, and this was one of those times.

Dick stopped the daily complaining, which helped a lot. His health seemed to have a miraculous recovery. He still has problems, and always will, but they are minimal compared to what I had been listening to for years. I think when he stopped complaining constantly, he actually began to feel better. He became more active than he had been for years. This only made me believe even more strongly, he is a hypochondriac.

Shortly after my return Dick had two surgeries on his cataracts. Thankfully his sister took him to those appointments. I hadn't seen or spoken to any of Dick's family since I left in July. Dick has gotten together with them, but has continued to exclude me, which is fine with me.

About six weeks after I returned home, my brother was hospitalized. He would be placed in the Compassionate care unit. The last time I visited him, he was no longer coherent. I just sat in the room as the nurses checked him, cleared his nose and throat and straightened his bed. As the nurse left the room, she stated, "You can talk to him, he can hear you." I knew Bud could hear me, but we had already said everything we had to say to one another. I stayed a short time, quietly observing my brother for the last time. As I left, I touched him on the shoulder and said, "I will see you." About one hour

O Holy Spirit, Enlighten Me

later his closest friend for the past few years called to say he had passed away. It wasn't unexpected. He had been seriously ill for some time. I only heard my brother speak of his pain two times. Each time was in the last two weeks of his life. He was aware of how tired I was of listening to my husband. I respected Bud for keeping his discomfort to himself.

I felt a long time ago my brother would be reborn to one of his estranged granddaughters and had shared this with him. His youngest son had severed his relationship with him many years ago. About a week before Bud's passing that son, his wife and two granddaughters would visit Bud. I knew it meant a lot to Bud.

I hadn't seen my brother's first wife for years. I ran into her at Bud's and she had a surprise for me. She said, "I know where your sister is." That was something I had asked God for years, "Where is my sister, Carol?"

Bud's ex-wife believes one of her granddaughters is Carol reborn. As soon as she said it, my body felt she was right. Although she thinks she knows which one is Carol, I haven't received that message from God. I, however, believe it to be the other granddaughter. When I am supposed to know which one is Carol, I will know. It is not time for me to know. But I do believe his ex-wife is correct, and one of the girls is Carol reborn.

As time passed Dick had more doctor's appointments, and I relented and took him to those appointments. My conscience won't let me inconvenience others any more than I have too. He seems so much better physically than he has been for years. At least I am not worrying about him passing away any time soon.

I am still struggling with Dick's personality. I can't remember what I found so attractive about him when I married him. That person disappeared a long time ago. I try to accept him as he is, but it is still a struggle. It has been an exceptionally charged political year, and of course, we don't see our politics through the same lens. I feel Dick is totally brainwashed and believes everything he hears on the station he listens to. To him, the Republicans do no wrong, and the Democrats do nothing right. I get upset with him and tell him, "You can't just listen to one side. Each side only tells you what they want you to hear. You have to listen to both sides and judge for yourself."

It is not yet Thanksgiving and I have many of my Christmas decorations in place. I would probably finish today, except I have Jenna and more than likely will tomorrow as well. Jenna has a cough and runny nose, thus she isn't at childcare. I enjoy my time with her and when she had a stinky diaper, I asked, "Where did this stinky diaper come from?" She so cutely pointed to her belly. She is so bright for her twenty-one months.

About six weeks after my brother's passing, he would speak to me one night. He apologized to me for something he had done years earlier and he asked how I was. I told him, "The past is the past, and I am fine." I have been communicating with the other side for years, but this was the first time I knew with whom I was speaking. It is usually just a voice, but this night two people spoke to me, and I knew who each of them was. The other voice was the husband of an acquaintance and someone I never met, but I knew who it was. Both conversations surprised me and once again God showed me His power. These things always amaze me, as they are so out of my control.

I was watching both of my granddaughters when I noticed Jenna had disappeared. I was just about to look and see what she was into, when Jenna came walking out of my bedroom. She had a big smile on her face and a chocolate covered mint in each hand. She had been in my room going through my drawers, looking for candy, and found the mints that I had actually forgotten were there. I went to retrieve the remainder of the mints when I noticed she had stomped one into my carpet. Jenna has a smile that just makes everything okay. I can't get upset with her.

A week later, Melanie needed a break and wanted to sleep in for a change, so I offered to keep the girls for the night. Looking for candy, Jenna once again made a dash for my bedroom. I peeked into my room to see what she was into and received the cutest guilty smile. I had moved the candy and she didn't find anything in the drawer where it had been.

As she left my room, she tripped over the rug and hit her head on the clothes hamper in the hall. She screamed, as she really hurt herself and received quite a bruise on her face. Melanie got her settled and left for the evening.

Shortly after Melanie left, I decided to put Jenna's pajamas on, as it is nearly bedtime. I laid her on the rug in my family room and found she needed a diaper change. As I went for the diaper, she wet herself into the rug. I got the clean diaper and pajamas on her, disposed of the diaper and was cleaning the rug when once again Jenna screamed. I ran to my room, where she had once again gone. She was standing in front of my dresser with the fingers on both hands closed in another drawer. I released her fingers and once again comforted her.

She is so curious and is really a handful, but I love her all the more for it. Not ten minutes later, she had a messy bowel movement. That was my first hour. Because of the head bump, I am trying to keep her awake for a little while. Eight o'clock can't come soon enough. I thought to myself, "No wonder my daughter needs a break. Jenna hasn't even reached two years, what are the "terrible twos" going to be like?"

The friend with whom I stayed in July fell and has been in a nursing home ever since. In the nursing home, she would contract the virus, but survived relatively no worse. She, like everyone else in nursing homes, is in quarantine. I had sent her an adult coloring book and when I spoke with her, I asked if she had colored any of it. She said she couldn't. We talked for about an hour and our reception was terrible, but I could tell she was having trouble remembering things. She said she didn't know how to use her phone. I often think of her and wonder how she can survive being closed in one room, day after day, with no visitors. I'm not sure I could cope with this very well. Even though she shares many of my husband's characteristics, I will be forever grateful to her for letting me stay with her when I needed a place to go.

The virus in our area is once again exceptionally bad, thus once again I haven't seen some of my friends for months. The weather has gotten cooler, thus we can no longer eat outside. I miss the opportunity to unwind and relax when I am with them. It was so hard on a few of them the last time we were quarantined, I hope they are enduring the isolation better this time. There are a couple of restaurants I feel are relatively germ free, and I don't feel confined, thus I do meet one or two of my closest friends about once a week at one of those restaurants.

As Christmas approached, I couldn't find the spirit this year. I sent my friends funny Christmas cards instead of religious ones. I feel we all need something to make us smile.

O Holy Spirit, Enlighten Me

It has been a very stressful year for so many people. Although a vaccine was recently approved, it won't be available to the general public for many months. I, like everyone else, will be glad when this virus is under control, and we can go back to our normal lives. I presently know multiple people who have the virus. Thus far, each is doing relatively well. It seems every time I speak with someone I hear of another acquaintance that either had, or presently has, the virus.

Although child care is still open, the holidays are approaching and school has been closed more frequently. The stress of constantly changing schedules is catching up with my daughter. Trying to work from home with two children present much of the time isn't helping. I continue to help Melanie with the girls as often as I can.

Although Dick loves to have the girls at our house, today the girls were fighting and got on Dick's nerves. He screamed at them and when I looked at him, he had that look of pure anger which has always upset me. His expression and tone are so ugly when he gets angry. I don't think I have ever seen this look around his friends, only when he is home with his family. It is times like this when I really want to go my own way, and not deal with his anger.

I was taking Dick to have a surgical procedure. We aren't going five minutes from our house. As I proceeded to turn right, he said, "Turn left, there will be less traffic." I thought, "It is 6:00 in the morning. There is no traffic in our area at 6:00 A.M." Without any change in my heart rate what-so-ever, I turned left and went his way. At the time, I felt I'd successfully crossed another bridge.

While the government is asking we limit our holiday gatherings, Melanie, Lance, the girls, Kelly, Dick and I had a very nice Christmas Eve at our house. The girls already have so many toys, it is hard to surprise or excite them with presents. We are fortunate, as we had plenty to eat, but I thought about all those who are experiencing the most disappointing Christmas in their lifetime.

The next morning when Dick left for church, our driveway and the roads are snow-covered. While he attends church, I am thinking of all the parents whose children woke up to few, or no presents under the tree this year. As I caught up with the news on the television, there are unbelievable lines of cars with people waiting to get food. It is so sad that the United States has fallen this far. I am so disappointed in our politicians and especially our president. This is not the way the world should be today. We are better than this.

Due to the virus, many churches aren't holding their normal Christmas service. I do not attend church. I don't care what others think if I don't attend church. I don't pray in the manner most people do, nor do I read the Bible. I simply have conversations with God on a daily basis, and I know He gets my messages, as He has answered me numerous times. I listen to my conscience, and do as I am guided. I am very content in my relationship with God. I know God understands me, and that is all that matters.

When Dick returned from church, we went to Melanie's. As we prepared to eat dinner, we said a prayer, ending it with "Amen". We were all enjoying dinner, when Jenna began singing the alphabet. She sang, "A-B-C-D-E-F-G, H-I-J-K-L-M-N-O-P, Q-R-S-T-U-V, W-X-Y-Z… Amen." Stunned at what we just heard, we all laughed. Jenna is only twenty-two months old. We were amazed she knew the entire alphabet, but the "Amen" at the end was too much.

Kelly had to work on Christmas day, but he would join us after he had finished for the day. We continue to include Kelly at our family gatherings. After a quiet day, we returned home and relaxed, listening to music again this year, as we had last year. One year ago, I didn't think I would be spending another Christmas with Dick. We had spent New Year's Eve day at the doctor's office and then the emergency room.

I have truly let go of Dick and my marriage this past year. I am ready to move on with my life. I am more aware than ever, no matter what the subject, Dick is going to disagree with me. It is so tiring and ridiculous. I am certain he doesn't even know he does it. I often avoid speaking with him, because I know where the conversation is going, before I ever say anything. I can't believe I have spent my entire life with this, and it took this long to feel unable to tolerate it any longer.

I often ask God, "What has the past couple of years been about? I haven't felt Dick's passing for a couple months. I am hopeful I won't feel it again, but it is something over which I have no control. I remember the first time I felt the passing of someone, I felt it for years. At the time I didn't know who that person could be. I only knew it was someone close to me. It would be more than forty years before I lost my daughter, but when it happened, I knew immediately that was what I had been warned about. It could be twenty years before Dick leaves this life, but God has made sure that whenever that might be, I will have made peace with my relationship with him.

Chapter 31

I thought I was doing better at accepting my husband, but I was wrong. Sometimes I find it stressful just being around him. I moved a few of his belongings in the basement, and when he went down to look for something, I was surprised he hadn't noticed. I only moved things I knew he would no longer use, but if he had noticed there would have been words of anger, because I touched his things. When he discovers I moved things, I don't want to hear his angry words.

As I went through his belongings, I started counting some of the items. I found he owned more than 25 guns, 2 compound bows, 9 pair of boots, 8 camouflage hunting suits, 8 gun cases, 8 turkey decoys, 4 duck decoys, 2 deer decoys, and 10 padded seats, on which to sit, while he was hunting. This was only a portion of the items he owns. I don't care he has all these items, except I remember so vividly, what I heard every time I spent money for anything. God is not making my road an easy road.

O Holy Spirit, Enlighten Me

I know Dick is trying to get along, but I can't forget the last fifty-seven years of discontent. Our anniversary is next week. I wish I thought it was an accomplishment to have been married fifty-eight years, but I don't feel it to be an accomplishment at all.

When I went to bed I could hear the water running in Dick's bathroom. I thought perhaps he was taking a shower and I went to bed. When I got up a few hours later, the water was still running. I went into Dick's room, he was sound asleep. The water at his sink was running, and had been for hours. He has done this three or four times. Instead of being upset, I am beginning to feel sorry for my husband.

It has been many, many months since Dick scared me with his driving. Still, I will not get into a vehicle with Dick driving. Knowing he won't use common sense, when he has a problem, has taught me a lesson. Unless it is an absolute emergency, I don't ever want to be in a vehicle with him behind the wheel.

Recently a friend made the comment to me that I hate my husband and I could change my life. I told her, "No I can't. The last time I was seriously considering leaving my husband, I woke up with blood in my bed. That was when the voice said to me, "He died for you."

I went on to tell her, "No, I don't hate my husband, nor do I want him to die. I just no longer want to be with him." In a perfect world Dick would accept our marriage is over and we could peacefully go our separate ways. But in reality, Dick has never been good at accepting change, or even admitting to himself, we are just not compatible. I want to tell him the only thing we have in common is we brought three children

I. M. Free

into the world and our home, but I try not to upset him, and I really do not want to hurt him.

Dick was listening to President Trump speak at the rally that preceded the insurrection of our U. S. Capital. As Dick listened, what I heard was disgusting to me. I said to Dick, "How can you listen to this?" Of course, he got upset with me for saying anything about it. I left the room. A short time later, I turned on the television in the front room. They were showing the rioters entering the Capital. No longer watching television, I told Dick what was happening, "They are trying to take over the Capital. He didn't say anything. I went on, "Why am I telling you? You don't care. If you were there, you would be one of them." What I was watching made me sick to my stomach.

Even after watching President Trump's speech, prior to the attack, my husband would not condemn what was happening. It made me angry at him. I thought, "He is so blind." Once again, it made me want to get away from him. I want to be with someone whom I can share my feelings, and not end up in an argument.

Later in the day I cleaned his bedroom. His dresser is completely covered with medication bottles, papers and a television. I wanted to dust the top of the dresser, but knew if I didn't return each and every item in the same order, I would get screamed at. I decided not to dust the dresser.

This morning Dick had a colonoscopy. I took him, dropped him off and returned home. I wanted to hang a couple pictures I had purchased recently. If I had put nails into the wall and Dick heard me, he would have been angry that I was putting holes in the wall. I am so tired of living this way.

O Holy Spirit, Enlighten Me

That evening, I picked up dinner at a restaurant Dick and I used to frequent. On the way home my mother's address unexpectedly appeared on my GPS. The address was exactly the same as my mother's, except it was northwest, and my mother's address was southwest. When my daughter called, I told her about my mother's address appearing on my GPS. I said, "I know this is a message from God, but I don't understand the message." I went on, "I don't know how long I am going to be able to listen to God. Being in the house with Dick on a daily basis is upsetting." Some days it feels intolerable. I am beginning to feel there is no easy, painless way to end a marriage.

Before I went to bed I looked at my phone. A friend had called twice. I returned her call. She stated, as I usually call her back, she was worried something was wrong. I told her, "No, nothing is wrong. I am just in a terrible mood. I went on, "One year ago at this time I thought my husband wasn't going to be here much longer. It is one year later, and I am still dealing with the same things. I am seventy-eight years old, and I feel like I need my husband's permission to hang a picture. I just don't want to deal with this crap anymore."

Once again I am upset with God, because I am living with someone who doesn't make me happy, and I don't feel free to change my life. I don't want anything bad to happen to Dick. I just don't want to be a part of his life any longer. I would like to be myself, and not feel I have to do things his way, in order to avoid stress. I told God, "I just don't know how much longer I can continue to follow you. It is getting very hard to do. I would like to just come out and say, I want a divorce and move on."

That night God explained the reason for my mother's address to appear on my GPS. I am living the same life as my mother. My mother lived with exactly the same stress. Because Dick didn't drink I didn't see the similarities. The more I thought about it, the more I could see the similarities between my husband and my father. How could I have never noticed this?

God also explained to me, I see and feel things most people do not see or feel. I need to be more understanding and patient. God made my body feel the way I will feel one day, if I continue to be patient, and follow His guidance. The feeling was of a happiness, which I have never shared with my husband. I thought about God's message, and at least for the time being, it is giving me the patience to continue a little longer.

Saturday morning Kailee had her first basketball game. Melanie wanted to attend, but Jenna had the flu. Melanie asked if I would come over and stay with Jenna. Of course, I went. On Sunday, we were once again at Melanie's, watching a football game. While there, unwilling to serve himself, Dick asked Kailee to get him a glass of ice water. Kailee very nicely told him he could get it. Dick answered, "I don't know how." Kailee's reply was, "C-mon, I'll show you," and she walked to the water cooler. Dick got up and followed her. I love the wisdom I see in this six-year old.

About an hour after we returned home, I received a call from Melanie. Lance and Kailee are both throwing up, accompanied with diarrhea. Not the news you want to hear, when you have spent the last two days with the kids. The kids had been all over Dick and me, while we were there today. We can only hope Dick, Melanie and I don't get sick also.

O Holy Spirit, Enlighten Me

The next day, Monday, I didn't feel well all day. By evening it was clear, I also had the flu. I began throwing up and had diarrhea. I was in the bathroom, when I unexpectedly passed out and fell onto the floor. I remained in the bathroom, continuing to vomit and have diarrhea, and minutes later, passed out a second time. I would spend the night going back and forth between my bedroom and the bathroom. By the next day, the vomiting would cease, but the diarrhea remained. It was our 58th anniversary and I was pretty much confined to bed.

Instead of asking if he could do anything, Dick sat in the kitchen and worked on a puzzle. I occasionally joined him for short periods of time. As it is our anniversary, about 2:00 P.M Dick asked if I wanted lobster for dinner. I thought to myself, "You have to be kidding." I laughed inwardly, as he would have expected me to go after the lobster. When I didn't get upset, I realized how far I had come in dealing with my husband, as he really was. I realized, this was just who I married. It would be more than a week before I felt like myself once again.

Dick has spent seventy-five percent of his life disagreeing with me on most everything. When I think how different our lives could have been, had he only opened his mind and accepted, I also have a mind of my own. It was not up to me to live exactly as he wanted. Dick wasn't ready to be a husband. He needed a mother and this was what I ended up being. He is a good person. He has a good soul, but he has a lot of maturing to do, and not enough years left to do it.

Dick was so certain I had spent his money on publishing my book, he has been brooding about it ever since I had it published. This morning, I asked him if he knew why we had two savings accounts. Of course, he didn't. I told him, "The second account was the money I received from my mother's estate. I never spent it." Dick didn't have anything to say. He just left the room. I had never withheld that savings account from Dick. He knew about it. It was in both of our names.

When I got up the next morning, I noticed Dick had gotten up during the night, and left the kitchen light on. This morning, he tried to make toast, and the toaster wouldn't work. When I looked at the plug, he had only one prong of the plug in the outlet.

Chapter 32

After more than one year of keeping a diary of my life with Dick, I decided I didn't really want to write about my life any longer. I had written what I had hoped to be the end of my book. When I tried to forward the writing to my publisher, the computer kept shutting down and wouldn't let me write a note or send a message. After several attempts, I decided God wasn't finished with me. I may have believed I was finished, but God had different ideas. I realized He wasn't ready.

People walk out on marriages every day. Why can't I? I feel my life is just the same old repetition day after day. When I went to bed, I asked God, "Why am I writing this book? What is the purpose?" It often upsets me. I don't understand why I am doing this.

I should remember to ask God more often because that night, I received an answer. I understand why God recently pointed out to me how much alike my father and husband were. God explained Dick is beginning to understand where the money has gone. It was something I had told Dick for many, many years, but he never heard or understood. I swear it went in one ear and out the other. Just as Dick couldn't see where our money was going, I hadn't noticed how much my marriage mirrored my mother's. It was plain as day, but I hadn't seen it. I may have felt I understood my husband, but clearly, we both still have lessons to learn.

I always felt my father abused my mother. I never looked at the way Dick treats me as abuse, but the more I thought about it, the more I realized that is exactly what it was. Dick would never admit to himself or anyone else that the way he acts is abuse, but it actually is.

I need only concentrate on the patience I will need until spring arrives and I can once again be outside doing things in the yard. I will have days when I think I can't do it, but I will continue to listen to God and take life one day at a time.

The girls are my inspiration. I love being with them. I am very fortunate as I don't feel my age and I can still wrestle with them on the floor and we laugh and enjoy one another's company. At Christmas time, I had purchased some outdoor toys for them, which we will install in the spring. Kailee has made friends with the children next door and enjoys playing with them. This year, Jenna will be able to join them.

Melanie is working today, so Dick is going with Lance to Kailee's basketball game. I was watching Jenna. I decided to do my morning dishes when I realized Jenna disappeared. I called and looked for her in each room and didn't find her. As I returned to the family room, she was squatted behind Dick's recliner. I knew immediately what she was doing. Jenna hides when she does her business. I got a diaper and changed her. When finished, I asked, "Do you feel better?" With a smile on

O Holy Spirit, Enlighten Me

her face, she so cutely shook her head up and down. I get the biggest kick out of her personality. She always has an answer for me. I think it's time for me to invest in a potty.

That evening, Kris called while we were eating dinner. I returned her call when I had finished eating. A few months earlier, Kris and I were talking about reincarnation. I could feel where Kris was going with the conversation before it came out of her mouth. I tried to stop her, but she wouldn't be stopped. She said to me, "Dad is going to be your brother in your next life." It was something that had crossed my mind previously, but I had always done my best to block it out. I answered her, "If it is that way, I better be bigger than him, so I can beat the crap out of him." We both laughed about the entire conversation.

Today as we talked, I told her I wanted to take things from the basement and put them in the garage, as they are things we will never use again. I knew if I said anything to Dick, he would be angry. She said, "Just go ahead and do it." I answered, "I really can't take any more of Dick getting angry about what I want to do. It will just have to wait."

Weeks later, we received a deposit to our checking account from the Federal Government. Most American citizens will receive $1400. It is a check from the government to stimulate our economic struggles caused by the pandemic.

I had spent the last two days working outdoors. After picking up the winter debris from the lawn, I proceeded to the flower beds. I decided I would spend a portion of my $1400 on replacing the cushions on my outdoor furniture. The cushions I have are about twenty years old.

When Dick asked what I was going to do, I replied, "I am going to look for new cushions for the outdoor furniture."

I. M. Free

I knew exactly what his response would be, so I was mentally prepared. His response was, "There is nothing wrong with the ones we have." I answered, "No, but I have looked at them for more than twenty years. I want to look at something new." Living with Dick is like living with a broken record.

I did purchase new cushions but returned them as they didn't fit my furniture correctly.

I had ordered pillow covers online and when they arrived, I knew Dick was wondering how much I had spent on them. When I walked into the kitchen, he was studying the packing they had come in. He threw it down when he saw me. I am certain he was looking to see if the price was on the package. This is exactly the type of thing that has driven a wedge between us since the very beginning.

A few days later, I celebrated my seventy-ninth birthday. Kelly had purchased a lottery ticket for me and it was a $100 winner. I decided I would buy myself a new pair of shoes with the money. When I told Dick I was going to cash the ticket and buy myself the shoes, his immediate response was, "Don't you have enough shoes?" I was immediately upset with him. I asked him, "Can't you ever say, 'Okay, you deserve it. Go ahead and buy yourself something.'" I went on to tell him, "Our entire marriage you have had a problem with me every time I spend money." He had a look of hurt that I answered him the way I did. That made me even more disgusted with him. It is always, "Poor me" with Dick.

It has been a couple of weeks since I told Dick the money in the second savings account was from my mother. It seems his attitude toward me has changed significantly. I am questioning whether the difference I am seeing is due to the knowledge it wasn't his money I spent, or if God made him

O Holy Spirit, Enlighten Me

easier to live with because He knew I was getting very tired of Dick's attitude toward me. This is one of those things I will never know for sure, but the idea that Dick has been so unpleasant to me because of money only makes me want to walk away even more. It is so hard for me to understand how money can make such a difference to someone.

I don't want to continue living with someone that brings me down the way Dick does. He is always so negative about my life choices. The other night, I was upset with God because I don't feel free to walk away. All I did was give myself a terrific headache. As soon as I got over my anger at God, my headache disappeared.

Dick and I were eating lunch when I picked up a letter we had received regarding cremation. Dick had contacted the company months ago but never followed up because of the virus. I asked him what he wanted to do regarding the subject. He immediately called and made an appointment to speak with a gentleman. When the man came to the house, we purchased a cremation plan for Dick. Obviously, God guided Dick to do this, as Dick seldom plans anything, and there was absolutely no pressure whatsoever from me. A few days later, when the urn that came with the plan arrived at the house, Dick had no idea what it was. He asked, "Where is yours?" I answered, "I'm not going anywhere for twenty-five years, I didn't purchase one."

Jenna once again isn't feeling well and is spending the day with me. I was in the bathroom doing my hair when Jenna began unrolling the toilet paper. I asked her not to do that and wound it up again. Once again, she unrolled the toilet paper. For the second time, I rolled it back. When she proceeded to once again unroll the paper, I raised my voice and said to her, "I asked you not to do that." She instantly froze. She didn't move, didn't look either way. She just stood there, frozen. I went on and said, "I know you don't like to hear the word 'no,' but sometimes, when someone older than you tells you not to do something, you need to listen." She remained frozen. I said to her, "I love you." Still, she froze. I hugged her and said once again, "I love you." She turned her head to me and had the cutest smile on her face. Things were okay once again.

When she stood there frozen, it reminded me of the times my father would yell at my mother. I felt I could understand why my raised voice was upsetting to Jenna. I know how I feel when Dick hollers at me.

Remembering God's message of not letting Dick upset me, I have been concentrating on letting go of my anger toward Dick and the way our marriage has gone. I have learned not to react in the same manner. I simply remind myself, "Don't let him upset you." As a result, I feel more relaxed. Although I react differently outwardly, in my heart, I haven't forgiven him, and I know that is what I must next learn to do.

I do try to understand why Dick is the way he is. I actually often feel sorry for Dick. I think about how he was raised. Where would he have learned to be a good husband and father? I have been told his parent's marriage was turbulent and his father died while Dick was still in high school. I certainly don't blame his mother as she struggled just to keep her family together. My childhood was similar to Dick's, but I learned from what I have experienced as a child. I don't think most people even think about it.

In the past few months, I have seen small improvements in Dick. When it comes to caring for our home, he has been a free spirit most of his life. He has never seen how much work it takes to keep our home in the condition it is in. He usually doesn't see what he could do to help. This past year, Dick has regularly made his own bed, has occasionally taken the trash to the bottom of the driveway, and now recently cleaned up after himself at the dinner table. That was a real shock. Maybe there is hope he will waken even further before his days in this lifetime are over.

One lesson I have learned from Dick is you cannot reach or reason with a closed mind. The more I tried to explain something, the tighter he closed his mind. It became easier to just accept he has a closed mind and move on. He was not ready to hear what I was trying to explain.

I am certain once a person truly finds God, you can't close your mind to Him, at least, not for long. I am so glad I hear God and have learned to follow His guidance. I only wish I had that knowledge many years earlier.

I am not certain where God is guiding me. I can only take life one day at a time and react accordingly. God can make the unbelievable happen, I know that. But in all honestly, I don't believe I will be with Dick forever.

Chapter 33

I am aware all I have done the past few years is complain about almost everything Dick has done. I wish I could see a positive side to our marriage, but if I am to be honest, I can't see anything positive about being married to him. How can I continue to love and respect someone who has never been able to share his feelings about life? Dick has never wanted to listen to what I am feeling or been interested in what I am doing. I can't hang on to love forever when there is no communication. I don't feel I have a connection with him. He has no plans for the future. He just exists and is satisfied with his life. Today, I wouldn't want to take a vacation with him. Going on a vacation with him wouldn't be much different than going alone. Of course, I don't need to worry about that anyway, as he never even thinks about taking a vacation.

I recently once again lost patience with Dick over a remark he made regarding the money I spend and I told God I just didn't know how much longer I could continue to follow

O Holy Spirit, Enlighten Me

Him. I haven't gone anywhere except to lunch with friends and I have spent very little money with the exception of the normal household expenses. My life is so repetitious, and I realize I am tired. Sometimes, I just want to close my mind and do my own thing. But, because of my grandchildren and believing one day I am going to feel complete happiness, I continue to follow God.

God must have believed me because after telling Him one more time I didn't know how much longer I could follow Him, I began to see Dick attempt to be less disagreeable with me. We are actually beginning to live a somewhat normal existence. We still get upset with one another, but the hostility is less frequent. My life doesn't seem as intolerable as it did. I really needed this lack of tension. I haven't changed my mind in regards to how I feel about him, but I know I don't have a choice and this has to be sufficient for the time being.

A gentleman has been calling me for several months regarding, "I Don't Have Time." I never answered or returned his calls. I have realized for some time Dick feels threatened about anything regarding my first published work.

Months ago, I did read an e-mail to Dick. The e-mail was in regards to making a movie about my book. Dick's immediate response was, "Yeah, make a movie about it. It's all about me." Meaning, he believes it is all about him. I thought, but didn't say out loud, "No, the second book is about you." Instead, I replied, "No, actually it's about me, my pain, and losing my entire family. And, you should have been a better person." He then stated, "They only want your money."

I haven't taken or returned any phone calls pertaining to "I Don't Have Time" since I returned last fall. I never talk about my first publication. It just causes more tension at home. Thus, Dick believes the book is forgotten and no longer a threat to his life. Unknown to Dick, I am under contract with my present publisher, so I have no reason to return any calls.

One evening, I was going to send an e-mail to the gentleman who has been calling regularly for months. As I was preparing the e-mail, my phone rang once again. It was the gentleman. This time, I answered and explained to him I was just trying to send him an e-mail. Dick was gone at the time. I explained my situation to him and once again stated I will not talk about my book in front of my husband. After speaking with him, I knew it was not time for me to proceed with what he was offering.

I continue to ask God, "Why am I writing this book?" I don't have a clear understanding of the purpose. I know I am growing as a person. But why share it with the world?

Shortly thereafter, I awoke one morning, and had I not already sent my transcript to my publisher, I think I would have thrown the entire transcript into the trash. I had done that with my first writing. For me, it is my way of making a life I don't really want to think about, go away. I feel I have learned from my experiences, but my experiences are not something I like to dwell upon. Once I have learned what it is I was to learn, I want to put it into my past and move on. God must have known I was going to feel this way one day. Was that why He had me forward it to the publisher when I did?

I was in this frame of mind when I decided to print some recent family photos. Instead of the family photos downloading, a video of Tina began playing on my computer. The video is approximately ten years old. Tina is sitting on the

O Holy Spirit, Enlighten Me

floor and Melanie's new puppy is licking her face all over as Tina giggles. It is a precious video to me.

I knew this was a message from God. He was letting me know He understood and there is a purpose for what I am experiencing even if I don't yet understand. God always finds a way to let me know He is there.

Last week, Dick celebrated his eighty-third birthday. Kelly took Dick and me out to dinner. Melanie and Lance had made previous plans. They would celebrate Dick's birthday on Sunday when Melanie had us over for dinner.

I had purchased a birthday card for Dick. The front of the card was a picture of a mule with a 75% off sign. The card said, "I know how you love a BARGAIN . . . open the card . . . So I got you this CHEAP-ASS CARD! (Pretty good deal, huh?) Happy Birthday." It really wasn't a cheap card, but I felt it was so appropriate. I think Kelly and I enjoyed the card more than Dick.

I can't purchase a card that says what a good husband he has been or that I love him. It would be so hypocritical. I don't feel that way.

I have learned to take life one day at a time. I can never love Dick as I did when I married him. He has done too much for me to ever feel comfortable sharing my innermost feelings. I have no desire to be that close to him. Dick has been so much easier to live with the last few weeks. It has made it easier to forgive him for the way he has made me feel for years. I continue to live with him, living day to day, knowing that for me, this marriage is over. I still want to move on.

I believe I have learned what God was waiting for me to learn. I faced my life as it was. Then as God guided me, I learned not to let the things Dick does upset me, although inside I was still carrying anger about the past. I then learned to let go of the past and forgive him.

All I can do is remain honest with myself, take life one day at a time, and know it is going to be the way it is supposed to be.

My hope for the future is to live in a world where everyone does not feel the need to have a gun to protect himself. A world where you can stand or kneel for the National Anthem, as long as you respect the country in which you live, a country where people can feel free to love whomever they want, whether they are the same sex or not, where the color of your partner's skin doesn't matter, where we can worship freely without fear, where the Republicans and Democrats can work together to make our country a better place.

I hope to see the day when our politicians begin to once again think about what is good for the country, not just their party. Many of our politicians act like adult children, thinking only of themselves and their party. That is not why they are in Washington.

I have always believed the USA has been successful and powerful because the United States cares about the world, not just the United States. The United States has always supported helping other countries when they needed help. We are all human beings, whether we live in a poor country or a fluent country.

God tests us in so many ways. Do unto others, as you would have them do to you, as sooner or later, you will walk in the other person's shoes. If you don't understand something, one day, God will put you into a position where you will learn to understand.

I would like to thank David Cole for his encouragement and getting me started; Marcus, my marketing consultant who did his best to get my first edition noticed; April, who made me look smarter than I am by doing the editing; my doctor, for keeping me healthy and never suggesting psychiatric help; my friends, the majority of whom don't believe me but bring joy into my life, and my family who pretty much ignore my writing and keep me humble. But most of all, I thank God for putting all of these people in my life.

www.ingramcontent.com/pod-product-compliance
Lightning Source LLC
Chambersburg PA
CBHW021424070526
44577CB00001B/40